A FAITH FOR ALL SEASONS

To Reid,

With deep gratitude for
your friendship and support.

A FAITH
FOR ALL
SEASONS

Liberal Religion
and the
Crises of Life

William R. Murry

River Road Press
Bethesda, Maryland

Cover design by Barbara K. Lewis

Published by River Road Press
6301 River Road
Bethesda, MD 20817

Library of Congress Catalogue Number: 90-84573
Printed in the United States of America

fourth printing

ii

**To Barbara, Brian, Jonathan and Christopher
my family**

CONTENTS

ACKNOWLEDGEMENTS

Permission to publish material from the following sources is hereby gratefully acknowledged:

John Ruskin Clark, for excerpts from THE GREAT LIVING SYSTEM, copyright © 1977, published by Skinner House.

Max Coots, for a selection from SEASONS OF THE SELF, copyright © 1971, published by Abingdon Press.

Governor Mario M. Cuomo for a selection from his commencement address delivered at Iona College in June of 1984.

Harcourt Brace Jovanovich, Inc., for selections from WIND, SAND AND STARS, by Antoine de Saint Exupéry. Copyright © 1939 by Antoine de Saint Exupéry and renewed 1967 by Lewis Galantiere, reprinted by permission of Harcourt Brace Jovanovich, Inc.

Houghton Mifflin Company for excerpts from J.B.: A PLAY IN VERSE, by Archibald MacLeish. Copyright © 1956, 1957, 1958 by Archibald Macleish. Copyright © renewed 1986 by William H. MacLeish and Mary H. Grimm. Reprinted by permission of Houghton Mifflin Company.

Richard S. Gilbert for a portion of his poem "To Savor the World or Save It" from THE PROPHETIC IMPERATIVE, copyright © 1980, published by the Unitarian Universalist Association.

John H. Nichols for selections from his Minns Lectures, LIBERAL RELIGION'S RESPONSE TO LOSS.

Simon and Schuster, Inc., for excerpts from WHEN ALL YOU'VE EVER WANTED ISN'T ENOUGH, by Harold S. Kushner, copyright © 1986.

Viking Penguin, a division of Penguin Books USA Inc., for excerpts from THE GRAPES OF WRATH, by John Steinbeck. Copyright 1939 by John Steinbeck, copyright renewed 1967 by John Steinbeck.

The Westminister Press, for excerpts from ALL OUR LOSSES, ALL OUR GRIEFS, by Kenneth R. Mitchell and Herbert Anderson, copyright © 1983 by Kenneth R. Mitchell and Herbert Ernest Anderson.

Preface

No religion is worthy of its name unless it provides a vision of meaning and purpose for the individual's life and help in times of personal crisis. Unitarian Universalism has been accused of failing to provide these. It has been called a fair weather faith, beneficial to its adherents on sunny days, but not helpful when the days are overcast.

I have written this book to refute that view and to offer some answers to the deepest and most perplexing questions that confront us: the problem of why we suffer pain, loss and death and the religious resources available to help us cope with these; and the search for a meaning and purpose in life that transcends the self. Each crisis is discussed as both a theological or intellectual problem and as a personal or practical concern. Thus the book deals with such questions as, "What meaning and purpose can life possibly have for us today?" "Why do bad things happen to good people?" and "What resources does the liberal religious community offer when we suffer loss?"

My response to these crises represents one person's view arrived at over many years of questing and questioning. They are not of course the only answers possible from a creedless, liberal religious perspective.

Two words about language: First, because I am convinced that language affects as well as expresses thinking, I am committed to the use of gender inclusive language and often have used both masculine and feminine pronouns together. But the repetition of "him or her", "himself or herself" becomes cumbersome, so sometimes I have used masculine pronouns only in one paragraph and feminine pronouns in the next paragraph or vice versa.

Second, it is common to use the term "religious liberal" to refer to those of us who are liberal in our religious views. However, since the noun is "liberal" and the adjective "religious," the literal meaning of the term is a (social or political) liberal who is religious. Although I have used the phrase intending the commonly accepted meaning, I am not entirely comfortable with it. So, at the suggestion of the Reverend Alice Blair Wesley, I have also used the term "the liberally religious" in place of "religious liberal." While this phrase is more accurate, it is not yet a commonly used phrase and may at first seem awkward.

The opportunity to collect these thoughts and put them together in this form came from a five-month Sabbatical generously granted me by my congregation, the River Road Unitarian Church of Bethesda, Maryland, and I want to thank them for it. It was also their enthusiastic response to the topics of this book presented in the form of a series of sermons that encouraged me to prepare these essays for publication. I want especially to thank Barbara Lewis for her beautiful cover design, Dorothy Underwood who read an early version of the manuscript and made many helpful suggestions, and Sallie Toney for her superb editorial help.

I asked Alice Blair Wesley to read and evaluate the manuscript. She not only did that but in addition made numerous excellent editorial suggestions which have made the book more readable. I am more grateful to her than I can say. Finally, my wife, Barbara, read the manuscript in several versions and, as always, gave me much useful help, advice and encouragement.

PART I

THE NATURE AND RESOURCES
OF A
LIBERAL FAITH

1

INTRODUCTION:
NOT ONLY A FAIR WEATHER FAITH

> Religion is our human response to the dual reality of
> being alive and having to die.
>
> F. Forrester Church

Religion and Life's Crises

The story is told that before the birth of Gautama, who
was to become the Buddha, his parents were told that he
would be either a great emperor or an extraordinary religious leader. Determined that his son become a great emperor, the father tried to prevent the boy from becoming
interested in religion by shielding his son from awareness of
old age, disease, and death. The father built three palaces
for Gautama, surrounded him with young, healthy atten-
dants and thousands of dancing girls, and made sure that
whenever he went riding, his path was cleared of any who
were ill or elderly or dying.

Even so, one day as he was out riding, the prince saw a
bald, toothless and feeble old man and asked what was
wrong with him. He was told that the man was simply old
and that when people become old they lose their hair and
teeth and become feeble. The next day the prince saw a
person suffering from an incurable disease, and he learned
for the first time that pain and suffering belong to the
human condition. The third day he saw a funeral procession,
and the young man learned the dreadful fact of death.

Deeply distressed by these revelations he asked: "How can life be happy and joyful if we suffer pain and illness and eventually become old and die?" Resolving to dedicate his life to a search for freedom from the miseries of old age, disease, and death, he embarked on a religious quest.

Anthropologist Bronislaw Malinowski wrote:

> Religion is not born out of speculation or reflection, still less out of illusion or misapprehension, but rather out of the real tragedies of human life, out of the conflict between human plans and realities.[1]

To qualify as a vital and viable religion a religious movement must deal with the tragedies of human life in a significant way. However, some have felt our Unitarian Universalist faith fails to do that. For example, several years ago the Religion section of *Time* magazine carried a story about a rabbi who, dissatisfied with Judaism, was seeking a religious affiliation more compatible with his modern scientific views. Asked if Unitarianism might not be the religion he was looking for, the rabbi replied that it was not, because Unitarianism did not deal adequately with the reality of death.

Recently a member of my own congregation who had lost her father wrote me to say that despite having benefited immensely from the life-affirming experience of participation in our congregation for several years, she was returning to the Roman Catholic Church of her childhood because Unitarian Universalists did not offer the answers she sought as she tried to cope with her father's death and the prospect of her own.

These evaluations may represent more than two isolated instances. Those of us who proclaim and practice liberal religion may sometimes have portrayed ours as a fair weather religion, a religion for the sunny days, not a religion for all seasons. My purpose is to make clear a liberal religious perspective on several of the important issues all of us face at one time or another. If Unitarian Universalists cannot speak adequately to these crises, then I would agree with our detractors that our faith fails us. However, this is not the case. A liberal faith does provide satisfying answers to the crises of life, specifically to the struggle for meaning and purpose, the problem of pain and suffering, and the crisis of loss and death.

To be human is to endure pain and loss and the separation of death — both separation from loved ones who die and finally our own separation by death from all that we love and enjoy. No religion eliminates pain, loss, separation or death from human life, and no religion prevents those realities from causing us suffering and grief. Unitarian Universalists, like other religious people, find in their faith a perspective that gives meaning to personal crises and comfort and strength in times of crisis. Religious faith does not of course eliminate the crises of life; it does reduce the anguish they bring and provides resources to cope with their impact.

To be human is also to question the reasons for and the meaning of suffering, loss and death. The answers of the liberally religious to these "why" questions are not the same as those given by the more traditionally religious, but they are both honest and satisfying.

It is sometimes said, perhaps in the interest of promoting a superficial tolerance or unity, that it does not matter what we believe. I disagree. What we believe shapes our attitudes toward life and our responses to specific events. What we believe about life and its meaning, about suffering, loss and death influences deeply how we live and what we do when we face these experiences. This book offers a liberal philosophical and theological perspective on these experiences.

Our faith has to offer us more, though, than an intellectual understanding in the midst of crisis. Equally important is the personal or pastoral dimension, the ministry of the religious community to those suffering loss. To be human is not only to think; it is also to feel, and an adequate religious response to life's crises will include a ministry to the emotional aspect of life. Our discussion includes a treatment of both the psychological dynamics of particular crises and the effective ministry of the caring religious community.

Humanist and Theist

Liberal religion addresses the crises of life from a perspective amenable to *both* an open but non-theistic humanism *and* a naturalistic theism. Non-theistic humanists doubt the existence of a supernatural Creator and hold that we are responsible for ourselves and for the world, that we are not to expect a supernatural power to intervene on our behalf or empower or comfort us in times of need. To this type of humanist the resources we have to sustain us are within the self and within the human community, and these are considerable and sufficient. Most humanists do not believe in personal immortality, and so a humanist response to the problem of death will differ from that of the traditional theist.

In the first half of the twentieth century, humanists tended to be dogmatic in their rejection of theism and insistence that humanity must learn to be self-sufficient. More recently, a new humanism has emerged which is compatible with some forms of liberal theism. I call it "open humanism," for although it seldom uses God-language, it is open to the mystery of life and to transcendence in life.

Humanists and liberal theists may make quite similar responses to the crises dealt with in this book.

Mystery lies all around us: the mystery of life itself, the mystery of the universe, the mystery of love and the mystery of human intelligence. Even with the great discoveries of modern science, there is still much about life and the world that we do not understand, cannot explain, and may never understand or explain. With Einstein the humanist affirms that awareness of that which is impenetrable to us is the source of true religiousness. And with Dag Hammarskjold, the open humanist agrees that

> God does not die on the day when we cease to believe in a personal deity, but we die on the day when our lives cease to be illumined by the steady radiance, renewed daily, of a wonder, the source of which is beyond all reason.[2]

The major components of naturalistic theism may be outlined as follows.

Naturalistic theism shares with non-theistic humanism the view that we human beings are free and therefore responsible for our own actions. Its God is neither a Calvinistic God who foreordains and predestines everything nor the God of the pietist who regards whatever occurs as the will of Deity.

The naturalistic theist maintains that we humans are responsible for the world as well as for our own individual lives. God does not violate human freedom to save us from our own mistakes or malice. The naturalistic theist agrees with Dietrich Bonhoeffer, the young German pastor and theologian executed by the Nazis for his involvement in the plot on Hitler's life. In his *Letters and Papers from Prison*, Bonhoeffer wrote that for many God was a *deus ex machina* to be called on in times of crisis to rescue them, as in Greek drama when the author of a play introduced a god to resolve an otherwise insoluble situation. Bonhoeffer insisted that God is not like that, but that God expects us to solve our own problems. Rather than being a cause for despair, response to this God is an incentive to discovery and growth.

For the naturalistic theist, God's role is somewhat like that of a magnetic field. It draws us toward the good, the true and the beautiful, or it inspires and empowers us to do the good. God's power is the attracting, persuading power of love, not the power of force or compulsion.

Feminist theologians have contributed significantly to a contemporary liberal conception of God by repudiating the male imagery traditionally associated with deity in the West. Male imagery implies a God whose power is the power of strength or force rather than the attractive power of love and beauty that would be associated with female imagery of the divine. Male imagery also suggests a dominant and authoritarian God who expects subservience and obedience whereas female imagery implies a deity who works with and cares for human beings and continually nurtures our growth and creativity.[3]

Moreover, the God of naturalistic theism is not a supernatural being separate from the world who acts upon the world from without, but a God who is immanent in life and the world. The liberal theist postulates a monism in which God is in some sense identified with the universe and the universe with God. This is not the traditional dualistic view in which God and the world are separate entities.

Since the only language applicable to God is symbolic and metaphorical, we acknowledge the limits of our ability to conceptualize and discuss this or any type of theism. However, symbols and metaphors can be helpful in pointing to the relationship of God and the world. For example, God may be understood as the Ground of Being (Paul Tillich); that is, as that Life in which all things are rooted and from which all things draw nourishment and sustenance. This type of imagery is also found in feminist theology which suggests the Earth Mother image.

Or, the relationship of God and the world may be thought of as analogous to the relationship between air and living things. God is like the air we breathe; it is everywhere, invisible, and that upon which we depend for life. (It is interesting to note that in both Greek and Hebrew the word for breath is the same as the word for spirit.)

While such metaphors are only very partial representations of the holy in life (they involve no moral dimension, for example), they offer images of God quite different from the traditional image of an all-powerful Father. The immanence of God or the identification of God with the world represents a paradigm shift now occurring in the way many people conceive of God. Evidence of such a shift can be cited from a number of sources, but I will mention only two.

Albert Einstein wrote:

> The religion of the future will be a cosmic religion. It should transcend definitions of God, and avoid dogmas and theology. Covering both the natural and the spiritual, it should be based on a religious sense arising from *the experience of all things as a meaningful unity.*[4]

In an extraordinary passage of *The Color Purple*, by Alice Walker, Celie and Shug talk about God. Celie has spoken of her rejection of a God she regards as white, male, distant, and unhelpful. Shug, however, has a very different conception:

> Here's the thing . . . The thing I believe. God is inside you, and inside everybody else. You come into

the world with God. But only them that search for it inside find it. And sometimes it just manifest itself even if you not looking, or don't know what you looking for. . .

It? [Celie asks]

Yeah, It. God ain't a he or a she, but a It.[5]

Then follows a passage in which Shug refers to her mystical "feeling of being part of everything, not separate at all. I knew that if I cut a tree, my arm would bleed. . . ."[6]

An important implication of this worldview for a theology that deals with life's crises is the inter-connectedness of all life and particularly of all humankind. Moreover, the God of naturalistic theism may be understood not as complete and unchanging, as in traditional theology, but, like all creation, as in process. God can be thought of as participating actively in the vast ongoing evolutionary process of the universe, pulling it toward maturation, or perhaps better, inspiring and empowering all living things toward the good.

God is that concept we use to point to the mystery and glory in and behind the universe and life, what Rudolf Otto called the *mysterium tremendum et fascinans*. The liberally religious, theist and non-theist, like all religious people, is filled with awe and wonder at the inexpressibly vast and beautiful universe in which we live. Such wonder leads to worship, and the liberal theist calls the object of worship God.

Postscript

Since individual freedom of belief is a cardinal principle for Unitarian Universalists, no one can articulate *the* Unitarian Universalist answers to the crises of life. My intention here is to articulate a liberal religious perspective I hope will have value for others as well.

Finally, I am told the Chinese ideogram for *crisis* has two parts. One part means *danger*; the other means *opportunity*." When we experience a crisis, we are in danger of having the foundations on which we have built our lives shaken and perhaps destroyed, but we are also confronted with an opportunity for growth. I hope this book will help the reader deal with the dangerous aspect of crises and also suggest ways in which the experience of crisis may be an opportunity for spiritual growth and maturation.

2

RESOURCES OF LIBERAL RELIGION IN TIMES OF CRISIS

What are the principal resources the religious liberal has at his or her disposal for dealing with the crises of life? This chapter will suggest some of these, and subsequent chapters will apply these resources to specific concerns.

For several years Antoine de Saint Exupéry flew a mail plane in the early days of flying when airplanes did not have today's sophisticated equipment. Saint Exupéry tells of one experience flying the route from Southern France across the Mediterranean Sea to North Africa. Night fell with the pilot and his radio operator, Neri, above the Sahara, and the radio messages sent from the ports in the desert concerning their position were clearly inaccurate. They suddenly found themselves far off course and low on fuel.

> We had no means of angular orientation, were already deafened, and were bit by bit growing blind. The moon like a pallid ember began to go out in the banks of fog. Overhead the sky was filling with clouds, and we flew thenceforth between cloud and fog in a world voided of all substance and all light. The ports that signaled us had given up trying to tell us where we were. "No bearings, no bearings," was all their message, for our voice reached them from everywhere and nowhere. With sinking hearts Neri and I leaned out, he on his side and I on mine, to see if anything, anything at all, was distinguishable in this void. Already our tired eyes were seeing things — errant signs, delusive flashes, phantoms.

The fliers' emotions suddenly went from despair to hope and joy as a point of light appeared on their port bow.

Assuming it was the light of an airport, Saint Exupéry began to bank the plane in the direction of the light only to see it twinkle and go out. They saw other lights, but with each their hopes rose only to be dashed as the light proved to be that of another star.

> . . . And with that we knew ourselves to be lost in interplanetary space among a thousand inaccessible planets, we who sought only the one veritable planet, our own, that planet on which alone we should find our familiar countryside, the houses of our friends, our treasures.

What a fitting and poignant metaphor of our situation in the midst of a crisis! We experience a feeling of being lost, groping in the dark, looking for a light to show us the way, and finding none, or perhaps like Saint Exupéry, finding first one then another, none of which saves. But the story continues.

Flying blind and often in dense fog, not knowing where he was but knowing he could not make his destination, Saint Exupéry now began to set his course so he would not have to come down at sea. Then suddenly the airport at Cisneros, their destination, made contact with them. They now knew the direction they needed to follow although they did not think they had enough fuel to get to Cisneros.

> But the airports one by one had been waking each other up. Into our dialogue broke the voices of Agadir, Casablanca, Dakar. The radio stations at each of these towns had warned the airports and the ports had flashed the news to our comrades. Bit by bit they were gathering round us as round a sick-bed. . . .
>
> And suddenly into this conclave burst Toulouse, the headquarters of the Line three thousand miles away, worried along with the rest. Toulouse broke in without a word of greeting, simply to say sharply, "Your

reserve tanks bigger than standard. You have two
hours fuel left. Proceed to Cisneros." [7]

Four points from this story suggest the resources available
to the liberally religious in times of crisis.

First, our own resources are often greater than we realize.
"Your reserve tanks bigger than standard." I believe this is
true of all us. We have reserves we seldom draw on and
often don't know are there. But they are. We have only to
reach down more deeply to draw on resources within ourselves.

I have seen this happen time and again. I think of a
woman whose husband was dying a long, slow death from
cancer. His gradual loss of physical, then mental capabilities
bore down physically and emotionally on her. Where she
found the strength to care for him and then after his death
to participate with me in planning a meaningful memorial
service, I can only guess. But I would say she drew on
reserves deep within herself.

I think of a dying man who faced his last months and
weeks with courage and grace and cheerfulness, determined
to live as well as possible until the end. I am sure he was
drawing on deep inner resources.

Some of us would say these people were strengthened by
God or that the power and grace of God at work in them
enabled them to carry on under trying circumstances. Others
would insist that they were simply drawing on human resources. The theist identifies the depth in our being with
God or the Creative Life Force; the non-theist does not.
Whatever we name it, the religious liberal can recognize and
acknowledge a deep reservoir within each person from which
strength comes in times of crisis.

Unitarian Universalists hold central a belief in the dignity of each person including oneself. With this goes a faith in one's ability to tap one's own deep inner resources, or, if you wish, to draw strength from the Power of Love and Creativity. This is very different from "toughing it out", from a kind of Stoic resignation and stiff upper lip attitude. What I am talking about has more of the character of grace. It involves the faith that life is good and worthwhile, though it is often unfair and includes pain and loss and ultimately death. It involves gratitude for what is, without bitterness or resentment for what is not and cannot be.

We usually think of faith as assent to a set of teachings for which there is little empirical evidence. But that is belief, not faith. Faith refers to a basic trust that life is good and worth living and that the context in which we live is gracious and trustworthy. To a person with this basic trust, life is a gift, a gift to be enjoyed and cherished and developed and used for the benefit of humankind. This basic trust cannot be demonstrated by reason; nor is it a doctrine. It is an attitude, a basic confidence in or loyalty to life, and a deep resource in facing the crises of life.

A second resource available to Unitarian Universalists is the caring community. In times of personal crisis we need the help of others, and we can depend on others. Saint Exupéry was saved by the efforts of other people who finally succeeded in making radio contact with him. Others were reaching out, trying to help.

Few of us can get through our most serious personal crises without help from others. No matter how deeply we draw on our own reserves or inner resources, we need the support, encouragement, advice, comfort, and reassurance of others. Sometimes we simply need another perspective, a new way of looking at things. And, perhaps most, we need the caring presence of others. Often there is little anyone can say or do to reduce the pain or sorrow we are feeling, but just to know that another person cares enough to visit with us or just to be there with us silently sharing our pain and grief — sometimes that is enough. It does not change the situation that brought suffering to us — nothing can do that — but it can bring comfort and solace. Albert Schweitzer said it well: "At times our own light goes out and is rekindled by a spark from another person."

Liberal religion is not only a way to look at things religiously, a theology; it also creates a caring religious community. Many times people who have suffered loss or experienced crisis in some form have told me how much their friends in the church meant to them during their most difficult time. In times of personal crisis there is no substitute for a caring community, for people ministering to one another. When Martin Luther proclaimed the priesthood of all believers he was surely referring not only to the idea that each person has direct access to God without a mediator but also to the fact that each of us can and should minister to others. The ministry of professionals is important (as a professional myself, I believe this with all my being!), but it is not a subsitute for the ministry of the laity. Both are needed.

Third, all of us sometimes operate with erroneous ideas that interfere with the satisfactory resolution of our difficulty. In Saint Exupéry's case, he was operating with at least two false ideas. He thought he had less fuel than he did, and he thought he was farther off course than he really was. So too we may think that our lives are without significance or that we cannot find joy after the death of a spouse or after divorce.

What we believe matters; what we think about an event or a situation influences how we feel and what we do in response to it. Our expectations play an important role in our attitudes. As long as Saint Exupéry believed he could not make it to Cisneros, he followed one course. When he learned that he had extra fuel and could make it, he changed course. If I believe that my life can be meaningful and of value only if I rise to the top in my profession or make a lot of money, I will live one way. If I believe that my life becomes meaningful because of daily acts of kindness and helpfulness, I will live another way. What we believe about suffering plays an important role in how we respond to suffering. What we believe about death influences our response when another dies and as we anticipate our own death.

So what we believe about these human experiences makes a difference in how we respond when we confront these matters. That is why much of this book deals with matters of belief, with theology.

I conclude this chapter with a final insight drawn from Saint Exupéry's experience which applies to us when we confront a critical situation in our lives. Even though Saint Exupéry was not sure where he was or how to get to his destination, he steered his course in the way that seemed best; he flew on in the hope that he would find the right course.

Sometimes that is the best we can do, too. In a difficult situation, unsure where we are or where we are going or how we can get there, we need not give up nor lose hope. Rather we can continue to steer our course in the best way we know in the hope and faith that it will soon become clear, that we will get through the crisis somehow. Sometimes all we can do is to "hang in there," with very little faith and very little hope, but with just enough that we don't give up on ourselves or that we don't despair.

At such times it is terribly important to be able to draw upon the faith of liberal religion that human life is sacred and worth living and that there are resources deep within which will sustain us and see us through. It is also crucial to have the support of a caring community. A liberal faith offers much by way of both insight and support when we face difficult times.

PART II

THE CRISIS
OF
MEANING AND PURPOSE

3

THE PROBLEM OF MEANING
IN THE MODERN AGE

We live not by things but by the meanings of things.
                              Antoine de Saint Exupéry

There is but one truly serious philosophical problem,
and that is suicide. Judging whether life is or is not
worth living amounts to answering the fundamental
question of philosophy.
                                          Albert Camus

The business of religion is meaning.
                                       Dean M. Kelley

Tall, good-looking and in his early thirties, Tim had just started coming to my church when he asked to see me. He got straight to the point. "I'm looking for a reason to live," he said. "I have a decent job; I make good money; I have friends and a woman I enjoy being with. But I have no direction, no purpose in my life. Making money and having a good time aren't enough. I want my life to count, but I don't feel that it does."

He went on to say that he had felt this way for as long as he could remember, but that he had previously buried such thoughts by keeping busy. Recently, however, his yearning for meaning and purpose had refused to stay buried. He had started coming to church hoping to find a spiritual foundation and direction. He could no longer believe in the traditional Christianity of his childhood and was looking for a religious philosophy that would make life worth living.

As I probed further, I concluded that he was quite stable emotionally, but felt keenly a void in his life that he wanted to fill. It seemed to me that he articulated clearly the situation that many people feel but do not always express. Many of us fill our time with busy activities which distract us from the awareness that our lives have little or no purpose or direction.

For Tim and for many people the search for meaning and purpose in life is neither an intellectual game nor a dispassionate exercise. It is a matter of life and death — not in the biological sense but in the spiritual sense. To find an answer is to be on the road to a life of satisfaction and fulfilment. To fail to find an adequate answer is to experience a lack of fulfilment and perhaps despair, what Kierkegaard called "the sickness unto death."

Albert Camus, in *The Myth of Sisyphus*, put it dramatically: "There is but one truly serious philosophical problem, and that is suicide. Judging whether life is or is not worth living amounts to answering the fundamental question of philosophy." [1]

Carl Jung believed the source of many of his patients' problems was meaninglessness.

> About a third of my cases are suffering from no clinically definable neurosis, but from the senselessness and emptiness of their lives. . . [T]his can well be described as the general neurosis of our time.[2]

Jung and Camus wrote in the 1930s and early 40s of a timeless human concern. I know of no one who has expressed that concern better in recent years than New York Governor Mario Cuomo who, at the Commencement exercises of Iona College in 1985, said of the graduates,

> They will have to decide soon the ultimate question — whether or not to live for *something*, or simply

> go from experience to experience, concerned about nothing more than what's in it for them. . . . They'll have to deal with the most fundamental question of all: *Why* do we make the effort? *Why* do we work? *Why* do we try? . .

Then, speaking of his own generation and the parents of the graduating class, he went on.

> Can we, who found the ultimate truth so elusive for so long, tell them with confidence now of the futility of gathering up riches and the things of the world?
>
> Most of us have achieved levels of affluence and comfort unthought of two generations ago. We've never had it so good, most of us. Nor have we ever complained so bitterly about our problems. The closed circle of pure materialism is clear to us now — aspirations become wants, wants become needs and self-gratification becomes a bottomless pit.
>
> All around us we have seen success in this world's terms become ultimate and desperate failure. . . . Entertainers and sports figures achieve fame and wealth but find the world empty and dull without the solace or stimulation of drugs. Men and women rise to the top of their profesions after years of struggling. But despite their apparent success, they are driven nearly mad by a frantic search for diversions, new mates, games, new experiences — anything to fill the diminishing interval between their existence and eternity. . . .
>
> Do you think they would believe us if we told them today, what we *know* to be true: That after the pride of obtaining a degree and maybe later another degree and after their first few love affairs, that after earning their first big title, their first shiny new car and travelling around the world for the first time and having had it *all* . . . they will discover that none of it counts *unless they have something real and permanent to believe in.*[3]

We human beings differ from other animals in that we need something to live for, as surely as we need food and water. It is not enough simply to live; we need some reason for living. St. Exupéry said it this way: "We live not by things but by the meanings of things."

Psychotherapist Viktor Frankl stresses the importance of finding meaning to one's life and documents its relationship to survival in his remarkable little book, *Man's Search for Meaning.* He tells of his experiences as a prisoner in a Nazi concentration camp. Referring to those spared from the gas chambers, he concludes that the men and women who survived the years of hard labor and terrible deprivation had something to live for, some higher purpose to their lives. Those who died had lost the sense that their lives were worth living. On the basis of his camp experience, Frankl founded a school of psychotherapy he calls *logotherapy,* or *meaning therapy.* Frankl believes that many emotional problems result from a failure to find meaning in one's life and that these can be resolved only when one discovers something to make life worth living.

Throughout history religion has given expression to the perceived meaning of human life. Indeed, a widely-accepted definition calls religion "the search for meaning and value." Religion has to do with finding something to live for, a cause or object of devotion to which to give oneself. In a book entitled *Why Conservative Churches Are Growing,* Dean Kelley has written,

> The business of religion is meaning. . . . By far the most important patterns for human life are the very biggest ones, which explain the purpose of existence, the nature of reality, the fate of the world, the character of the beings or forces that determine our destiny and how we can relate to them. These largest patterns of meaning are the subject matter of religion.[4]

By providing an overarching meaning in ultimate terms, religion makes sense of everything that happens to its followers and provides them a reason or reasons for living. If our child dies and we ask, "Why do bad things happen to me?" our religious faith should help us answer that question. When we question why we should keep on working day after day or why we should not just look out for ourselves and say, "To hell with everyone else!" our religion should give us an answer. Liberal religion also offers ultimate meaning and purpose for the lives of its members.

Before describing what a contemporary liberal faith gives us, let us look at the answers our western religious traditions have given in the past.

The faith of Israel was grounded in the idea that Yahweh God had chosen Israel as his people. Yahweh had made a covenant with them, if they followed his commands, He would bless them. The meaning of their life as a people consisted in obedience to their God. Later their purpose expanded to include the task of making Yahweh known to the rest of the world. Their purpose as a people was to be "a light unto the nations" as the prophet Isaiah put it, and each individual Israelite could view his or her life as meaningful insofar as he or she participated in this larger purpose which included the perpetuation both of the nation and its religion. However, with the conquest and dispersal of Israel by her neighbors, another myth became operative. God would send a Messiah who would re-establish the kingdom of Israel and restore the people to their homeland. In each case the meaning of life was bound up with the purposes of the Almighty and would be fulfilled in the future. The life of the individual attained significance by contributing to the divine plan.

Christian faith also set the individual's life in a larger cosmic context. For the Christian the meaning of life lay in doing the will of God who in turn made the individual's life meaningful because it was part of the divine purpose of creation and redemption, culminating in the future realization of the kingdom of God. Human life is meaningful because of its role in God's larger purposes, and each person finds both meaning in the present and hope for the future by following what he or she understands to be God's way.

For many today, the meaning structure provided by the traditional religions has broken down. For various reasons, the biblical world view and the traditional religious perspectives no longer command allegiance or offer satisfying answers to life's ultimate questions. Cut off from the anchor of traditional belief, many people feel adrift; they experience life as without meaning. Loss of a center for modern life gave rise to the movement known as existentialism, a response to the sense of inner emptiness, hopelessness and despair which many felt without the traditional meaning structure.

In his book *The Courage To Be*, liberal Protestant theologian Paul Tillich characterized what he called "the anxiety of meaninglessness" as the dominant problem of our time. Tillich said three types of anxiety seem to be intrinsic to human nature: the anxiety of fate and death, the anxiety of guilt and condemnation, and the anxiety of emptiness and loss of meaning. Some degree of each type of anxiety is part of the human condition, but in different periods of history one kind of anxiety seems to dominate. Tillich believed that in our epoch the anxiety of meaninglessness is most pervasive. He described it in this way.

> The anxiety of meaninglessness is anxiety about the loss of an ultimate concern, of a meaning which gives meaning to all meanings. This anxiety is aroused by the loss of a spiritual center, of an answer, however symbolic or indirect, to the question of the meaning of existence.[5]

Drawing on the ancient figure of Sisyphus, Camus depicted this modern experience. Sisyphus was a greedy tyrant condemned by the gods to push an enormous boulder up the side of a mountain. A punishing task, it was made worse by the fact that just as he got it nearly to the top, the boulder rolled down, and he had to start all over again. Sisyphus was condemned to this never-ending, purposeless task for eternity.

If Sisyphus depicts the human situation, it means that all we do leads nowhere. Life is without meaning or purpose. It is simply "the same thing over and over and over again."

Most of us would admit to feeling that way at times. We may experience our jobs as a treadmill; no matter how hard we work, we get nowhere. We may question the worth or value of our work, or our personal and family life may sometimes seem to be pointless. For most of us the meaning of our lives is not a problem when things are going well, but it concerns us when we experience some kind of difficulty, as when we lose our job, or our marriage falls apart, or one of our children gets in trouble, or death takes someone close.

This is what happens to television producer Mickey Sachs in the movie *Hannah and Her Sisters*. Early in the movie, we see Sachs, played by Woody Allen, working at a frenetic pace, producing shows, creating new shows, making a great deal of money and on his way to the top of the ladder of success and fame.

However, he has paid a high price for his life in the fast lane. His marriage to Hannah has failed; his relationship to their children is marginal; and he has no real friends. The Mickey we see at this stage is a man dashing around frenetically, quick to lose his temper, self-centered and ambitious. He doesn't really connect with people — not with his former wife, nor his children, nor his business associates.

But he has recently been bothered by the loss of hearing in one ear. He learns from his doctor that his hearing problem could mean he has a brain tumor. He must have more tests made, but these will take time and while he is undergoing the tests and awaiting the results, he confronts the possibility of his own death, apparently for the first time. Frightened, he imagines that he has an inoperable tumor and only a short time to live. Imminent death forces him to look at his life and to ask what its meaning and purpose have been or ought to be.

Haunted by the threat of death and the emptiness of his life, he is unable to work; so he leaves his job and devotes himself to searching for an answer to his question. He desperately wants to believe in God and in life after death, and to the bewilderment of his Jewish parents, he tries to convert to Catholicism. But his efforts fail; he cannot believe. He reads philosophy trying to accept the arguments for the existence of God, but that doesn't work either. He looks at other possibilities, but nothing satisfies him.

Then he learns that he has no tumor. This brings relief, but it does not give him peace. For he has been confronted with death and the question of the meaning of his life, and his life has been forever changed. He cannot give up his search until he has found a meaning to life that satisfies his deep need.

Many of us are like Mickey Sachs; not until we are shaken by some unexpected and shocking experience do questions of meaning intrude upon our daily routine. It is when we are confronted with a chasm between our expectations of life and its reality that we experience the crisis of meaning.

If it is true that the "striving to find a meaning in one's life is the primary motivational force in human beings," [6] then it is essential that liberal religion offer a spiritual framework for meaningful living, the kind of foundation sought by Tim, the young man whose concern for meaning began this discussion. A liberal religious framework is spelled out in the next two chapters.

4

WOODY ALLEN, *ECCLESIASTES* AND THE SEARCH FOR MEANING

> If we hope to live not just from moment to moment, but in true consciousness of our existence, then our greatest need and most difficult achievement is to find meaning in our lives.
>
> Bruno Bettelheim

When the meaning of our lives is not self-evident and when many of us cannot derive our sense of meaning from traditional religion, where and how do we find meaning? Let us look at Woody Allen's answer in *Hannah and her Sisters*.

One day in the course of his increasingly anguished search, Mickey walks the streets of the city until, exhausted, he goes into a theatre just to sit down, without even noticing what film is playing. The movie happens to be an old Groucho Marx film Mickey had seen many times, but this time it becomes a vehicle of revelation for him. As he watches the movie, he is overtaken by the feeling that life is good and worth living even if there is no God and no after-life. All that really matters is to be able to affirm the present, to enjoy living and to have meaningful relationships with others. He decides it is not necessary to believe in God and immortality for life to be meaningful. His views on these matters have not changed, but clearly *he* has changed from the frenetic, competitive television director he was.

Shortly after this experience, Mickey meets one of Hannah's sisters, a woman who has had difficulty finding herself, and he is able to help and encourage her in her latest endeavor, writing. Later they marry, and we see a new Mickey Sachs, a man who has found happiness, contentment and peace in a life centered on his family and friends. At the end we see a more relaxed Mickey enjoying his wife's success and finding meaning and satisfaction in human relationships.

The movie says several things I find important from a liberal religious perspective. It points up the emptiness of the lives of those who pursue fame and fortune, whose lives are centered on themselves. Secondly, the film depicts the redemptive function of pain and loss. They often shake the weak foundations on which we have built our lives and force us to seek more solid ground.

And finally the movie suggests that even when the traditional structures have crumbled, that does not mean life can have no meaning. Life's meaning is not simply a given, not inherent in life itself. But that is not a cause for despair. Rather, it represents a challenge and an opportunity, for now it is up to us to create or discover meaning. We are the meaning makers; we are the ones who make our lives worth living. Dr. Harry Emerson Fosdick, distinguished liberal Christian minister of a generation ago, put it this way:

> Nobody ever finds life worth living. One always has to make it worth living. All the people to whom life has been abundantly worth living have made it so by an interior creative, spiritual contribution of their own. Is life worth living? Most people seem to think that is a question about the cosmos. No, my friend, that is a question about the inside attitude of you and me.

The question is shifted away from the metaphysical to the existential. The quest for meaning is not a matter of discovery but a creative task. Moreover, there is no one answer to the question of life's meaning. For what will satisfy one person may not be sufficient to another. A noncreedal liberal religion will maintain on this matter, as on others, that each person must discern what makes sense to him or her. But reason and experience offer some guidelines as to how we can make our lives meaningful.

Unitarian Universalist minister Richard Gilbert suggests two possible responses to the search for meaning:

> I arise in the morning torn between the desire
> To save the world and to savor it —
> To serve life or to enjoy it —
> To savor the world or save it?
> The question beats in upon the waiting moment —
> To savor the sweet taste of my own joy
> Or to share the bitter cup of my neighbor;
> To celebrate life with exuberant step
> Or to struggle for the life of the heavy laden?[7]

I suggest that for our lives to be most meaningful, we need both to savor the world *and* to save it, or, as I would put it, to contribute to enriching the lives of others. Most of us lead very busy lives. Someone has said, "We are so busy making a living we don't have time to enjoy living." We set goals for ourselves which demand long hours and hard work, and if we reach one goal we set another, ever believing that if we just attain one more rung on the ladder, we will be satisfied. We are like the swimmer who swam the English channel but, instead of savoring that accomplishment, immediately began training to attempt to swim it in both directions. Some of what we do is worthwhile and valuable but some is not; some consists of fruitless efforts to make ourselves important or acceptable or to prove our worth or to try to exercise power and control over others.

Instead of constantly working or running or reaching for the next goal like Mickey Sachs, many of us need to learn to savor more of the moments of our lives. We need to learn, like Mickey, to enjoy the companionship and conversation of others. We need to learn, when it snows, to take time to enjoy the loveliness of the snowfall rather than cursing it because it disrupts our routine. We need to learn, in the spring, to take time to appreciate the flowers, and, in the summer, to walk in the grass in our bare feet; to play with our children or grandchildren; to let ourselves feel awe at the sight of a soaring bird or an airplane lifting off. "Life is a series of moments," wrote Corita Kent. "To live each one is to succeed." [8]

This is the conclusion of Rabbi Harold S. Kushner in his book, *When All You've Ever Wanted Isn't Enough*. Kushner draws upon the book of *Ecclesiastes* in the Bible to illustrate the futility of many of the options we choose in our attempts to make our lives meaningful. *Ecclesiastes*, he suggests, was written by a man who had tried to make his life worth living in several ways. He had sought wealth and apparently succeeded in making a good deal of money. But his wealth did not bring him happiness, for he writes, "God sometimes grants a man riches, property and wealth, so that he does not want for anything, but God does not permit him to enjoy it." (Ecclesiastes 6:2)

He gave himself to pleasure, but this too he found futile. Kushner notes that young people, feeling they have a lot of time ahead, can justify spending their time in pleasure, but as people grow older and become more concerned about whether or not their lives count, pleasure-seeking does not satisfy. Kushner writes, "Having fun can be the spice of life but not its main course, because when it is over, nothing of lasting value remains." [9]

If neither wealth nor pleasure could provide what Ecclesiastes sought, perhaps knowledge and wisdom would. He turns to the pursuit of learning. Again, he experiences futility, for he discovers that knowledge and wisdom are transitory. They do not guarantee contentment.

Finally in desperation the author of *Ecclesiastes* turns to religion. Perhaps by following the practices and teachings of his religion, he can find peace and serenity and the sense that his life is significant. But again he is frustrated. For the kind of religion he practiced consisted mainly of legal discipline and ritual. "He learns that even the highest level of piety cannot protect him from death and the fear of death, or from the oblivion to which death leads." [10]

Having tried all these paths and found them wanting, what is left? These four paths constitute the ways most people take. They represent the faiths of our time and apparently of every age. If they are futile, is there any hope that our lives can be meaningful? Kushner says that the author of *Ecclesiastes* provides an answer, and that answer is found in what we have called savoring life.

> Go, eat your bread in gladness and drink your wine in joy, for your action was long ago approved by God. Let your clothes always be freshly washed and your head never lack ointment. Enjoy happiness with a woman you love all the fleeting days of life that have been granted you under the sun. Whatever it is in your power to do, do with all your might. For there is no doing, no learning, no wisdom in the grave where you are going.[11]

This, Kushner suggests, is more than an "eat, drink and be merry" hedonism. It is the profound advice that our lives are meaningful to the extent that we can savor each moment and find in each relationship and each experience something precious. The meaning of life is not a question with one big answer, but with many little answers. We don't eat one big meal and expect never to have to eat again. So we should not look for one big meaning to life which, once discovered, will satisfy us for the rest of our lives. Instead, like eating three meals a day, we will find life's meaning by savoring many everyday experiences.

> Life is not a problem to be solved once; it is a continuing challenge to be lived day by day. Our quest is not to find the Answer but to find ways of making each individual day a human experience.[12]

Kushner's conclusion is similar to the Hasidic emphasis on discovering the holy in the events of daily living and to Martin Buber's teaching that religious living is a matter of hallowing the everyday. That is how Mickey Sachs finds meaning in his life, too, although his language is secular, not religious.

To savor each moment and each experience, to hallow each relationship, to make the most of every event — this is essential if we are to find life worth living. Does that seem obvious? Yet it is a way many of us find difficult to follow. We are products of a goal-directed culture. We are always looking ahead and planning the next task or accomplishment. In that way, we often fail to appreciate the present, to live in what Paul Tillich called "the eternal now."

We *can* find meaning in simple, ordinary human experiences of love and beauty. Like Mickey Sachs we can find meaning and purpose in our relationships with those we love. Our devotion to the care and nurture of our family can be a major source of meaning because it is in the family that we feel loved and needed, and it is in the family that we are able to give ourselves to others in meaningful ways. The countless day-to-day tasks connected with the nurturing and growth of our children, the joys and even the disappointments of sharing and supporting each other which a couple experience — these things help to make life worth living. I find, for instance, that if I can help one of my sons learn how to solve a difficult math problem or gain some insight into a book he is reading, I feel those moments have had meaning and purpose. These experiences fulfil some very deep biological and emotional needs which left unfulfilled can frustrate our sense of meaning and purpose.

The experience of being loved by someone else and of being needed by another person outside the family also helps to give meaning and purpose to our lives. A member of my church involved in one of our support groups recently told me how significant the experience had been for her. She said she went into the group to find help and support for herself during a personal crisis, but she soon found that the help she was able to give to others was even more important to her. It gave her a sense of meaning beyond her own individual concerns.

Painting a picture, singing a great choral work or enjoying a trip to an art gallery are meaningful experiences. They lift us out of ourselves and inspire us to mold the clay of our lives into something sublime. The ordinary experiences of our lives can be enough to give us a sense that life is worth living.

The intrinsic satisfaction of work is another source of meaning and purpose for many, far more important than the financial rewards of the job.

Personal growth is yet another way of savoring life and making it more meaningful. Mr. Sammler, in Saul Bellow's novel, *Mr. Sammler's Planet*, puts it succinctly when he says: "The spirit knows that its growth is the real aim of existence." [13] Not only is personal growth worthy in itself, but it also carries on our evolutionary development. The person who is consciously growing can feel satisfaction that his or her life has direction and value. He or she lives at a level deeper than the life devoted merely to material abundance and self-indulgence.

Jung wrote that the second half of life must concentrate on the growth of the self. Jung believed that the first half of life centers on gaining competence and mastery in a field of endeavor such as engineering or raising children. The second half of life must focus on the soul, the development of one's personal and spiritual life. If growth does not occur, Jung believed, the individual will not achieve a sense of fulfilment and completeness when death comes.[14] The so-called mid-life crisis which many experience lends credence to Jung's view.

Personal growth and self-realization provide an important dimension of meaning to my life. If it were not a major purpose of my life, I would feel an emptiness and a lack of direction. But I have to ask what value my personal growth has beyond my own satisfaction. I find that I want to grow, not only for my own sake, but so that I can be of greater service to others.

Similarly, if we look closely at the reasons people find meaning and purpose in their work, we will find that even more than from their ability to savor each moment and task, satisfaction comes from the fact that their work contributes to something larger than their own happiness. For, important as it is to learn to live in and savor the present, that is not enough. Here I part company with Rabbi Kushner. We need larger goals and purposes which give our lives a meaning that transcends the self. It is these larger goals or purposes that make our lives truly worthwhile, and which make it possible to savor the world. Dick Gilbert reminds us,

> What is that you say?
> To savor one must serve?

To savor one must save?
The one will not stand without the other?[15]

The eminent twentieth-century Protestant theologian H. Richard Niebuhr put it this way.

> It is a curious and inescapable fact about our lives, of which I think we all become aware at some time or another, that we cannot live without a cause, without some object of devotion, some center of worth, something on which we rely for our meaning. In this sense, all [human beings] live by faith because they are [human beings] and cannot help themselves. . . . We never believe that life is worth living, but always think of it as made worth living by something on which we rely.[16]

Life is made worth living by our commitment to and involvement in causes which contribute to human welfare and world betterment. It is when we are trying to "save the world" that our lives become meaningful. Only then can we truly savor life.

So, personal growth is important not merely as an end in itself, but as a way of making it possible for us to contribute more to our family and friends and to the larger communities of which we are a part. It is true, paradoxically, that we realize our highest potential selves only when we focus on some other goal than self-realization.

Those who find meaning and value in their work are most likely to be engaged in work that contributes in some way to a better world. Those whose jobs do not offer that kind of satisfaction or who may be retired can engage in voluntary activities which add meaning to their lives. I think of a business woman I know who spends a great deal of her spare time working in a soup kitchen. I think of a retired couple who have dedicated their lives to working for peace. I think of a man retired from government service who is working in the area of low-cost housing. Each of these persons will tell you that their lives take on greater meaning and purpose because of these volunteer activities.

Alfred Adler wrote:

> Every human being strives for significance, but people always make mistakes if they do not see that their whole significance must consist in their contribution to the lives of others. . . . *Life means — to contribute to the whole.*[17]

What we do for other people and the world as a whole makes our lives worthwhile.

Again Governor Cuomo states it well in the address quoted earlier. Having decried the emptiness of the values of so many contemporary people, Cuomo goes on to say:

> . . . the philosophers were right. . . . St. Francis, Buddha, Mohammed, Maimonides — all spoke the truth when they said the way to serve yourself is to serve others; and Aristotle was right before them, when he said the only way to assure yourself happiness is to learn to give happiness. . . . [They] knew the only way to be fulfilled and pleased and happy was to *give* instead of trying to get.[18]

As I reflect on my own life, the times most meaningful to me are those times when I have been able to help someone else, those times when something I have said or done has been of value to another, and those times in which I have participated in efforts to create a better world through social change. And as I think of those people I admire most, whose lives I look upon as most worthwhile, I think not of those who have amassed fortunes, but of those who have contributed beauty or wisdom, those who served others or increased social justice. Those who have centered their energies on themselves, whose sole purpose has been self-gratification, are not people I respect or wish to emulate.

And, when I think of works of art, music and literature, or of architectural masterpieces, or of philosophies, scientific discoveries, technological triumphs and advances in psychology, I realize that these are the contributions of others, many of whom are no longer alive. What survives of them are the contributions they have made to human life. Those who made no contribution left nothing behind, and so their lives have been lost. Perhaps that is the meaning of Jesus' parable in Matthew 25 where he says that those who gave food to the hungry, clothing to the naked, and so on, would inherit eternal life whereas those who did not would be condemned to eternal damnation.

Dag Hammarskjold put it this way.

> Only what you have given
> is salvaged from the nothing
> which some day
> will have been your life.

It is what we give rather than what we get, what we do for others rather than what we do for ourselves, that makes life worth living. This principle lies at the heart of a liberal faith. However, it may seem that only those who make some great contribution to our world can live meaningful lives. It is fine for the Dag Hammarskjolds, the Aristotles, the Alfred Adlers, the Martin Luther Kings, and the Mario Cuomos to say these things, but what about the rest of us who cannot make so memorable a mark on the world?

It is not necessary to become famous or to change the whole world to make a significant contribution to the welfare of others. There are ways all of us can help to ease someone's burdens. There are ways in which we can give help or encouragement to another. There are movements in which we can participate which might have a significant impact on our community, nation or world. In a word, we can find meaning and purpose in life through being part of the larger community of people working for the things that make life better, more beautiful, more just, more livable, and more truly human for all people. Life is worth living when it is used in the service of a cause or purpose greater than the self. And when it is thus used we discover, paradoxically, that such a way of life enriches our selves as well.

5

THE LARGER CONTEXT:
A THEOLOGICAL PERSPECTIVE

> I believe we are here to some purpose, that the purpose has something to do with the future, and that it transcends altogether the limits of our present knowledge and understanding... If you like, you can call the transcendent purpose God. If it is God, it is a Socinian God, inherent in the universe and growing in power and knowledge as the universe unfolds. Our minds are not only expressions of its purpose but are also contributions to its growth.
>
> Freeman Dyson

> All are parts of one stupendous whole
> Whose body Nature is and God the soul.
>
> Alexander Pope

It is important to put the liberal faith perspective on meaning and purpose in a larger context — the context of human history and even the entire cosmic process. This is the theological task or, if you will, the mythological task. I mean by mythological not something factually untrue, but images, stories and symbols which help us to make sense of our lives and also have the power to motivate us. Myths provide a context for both meaning and ethics.

Joseph Campbell, in that extraordinary Public Broadcasting television series with Bill Moyers, said we need a new myth to replace the Christian myth which has empowered and informed the Western world for two thousand years. I believe we are witnessing the emergence of such a new myth. It is a two-dimensional myth inspired by a modern scientific understanding of the universe.

The theory of evolution gives us the temporal dimension of the myth. This is the vision of all reality as a single whole in an ongoing evolutionary process. In contrast with traditional western religion, with its dualism of natural and supernatural worlds, this view posits one world, one unified whole. And, instead of conceiving the "truly real" as static and eternally unchanging, all things are in process. This new vision is found in the process philosophy and theology of Alfred North Whitehead and his followers, in the writings of the Jesuit paleontologist Pierre Teilhard de Chardin and physicist Freeman Dyson, in the work of Sir Julian Huxley, and in the work of Unitarian Universalist minister/ theologian John Ruskin Clark and many others.

In this world view the world is imperfect and incomplete. Humanity's task is to work toward its completion. As long as there is hatred, oppression, poverty, hunger, disease, ignorance, suffering and evil, there is work to be done. In doing the unfinished business of the great evolutionary process our lives find meaning and purpose. According to this vision, evolution involves three stages.

The first, or inorganic stage, saw the emergence and increasing organization of matter. There was the formation of stars, planets and galaxies, of mountains, seas and rivers. Physical and chemical interactions which produced these and which continue to cause them to change have been going on for at least six billion years and are still evolving.

In the second stage life forms emerged, at least on planet Earth. The process of natural selection produced increasingly varied forms of life. This organic stage culminated in the birth of mind and self-consciousness in human beings.

The emergence of mind and consciousness has brought about a qualitative change in the nature of evolution. No longer simply an unconscious process of natural selection, evolution can now be a conscious process, not only biological but psycho-social. We are aware that what we do affects the future, and it is our responsibility to create a better future. This third stage of evolution involves *moral and spiritual* evolution, advancement in psychological and behavioral understanding, advancement in social and political justice, advancement in knowledge and the arts.

We have reached the point where we can influence the evolutionary process significantly. To some extent we alter nature to accommodate ourselves as, for example, when life is prolonged by modern medicine. To an even greater degree we exercise control over our social, cultural and moral development.

With this capability comes responsibility for the enhancement of life and the world and reponsibility to shape the future more positively. At the psycho-social level humankind is the instrument of evolutionary progress through the advancement and application of knowledge and the arts. We are to be responsible toward the whole, toward the Great Living System or the Creative Process. It is our duty to respect the earth and its resources.

We are also responsible to others; we are to do what we can to improve their lives, economically, educationally, and politically. (In traditional terms, this is the ethic of love, meaning to seek the well-being of others.) Poverty, ignorance, and injustice all point up the unfinished nature of the world. By working to overcome these problems we can contribute to the psycho-social evolution of Life and bring meaning and purpose to our lives as well.

And we are to be responsible to and for ourselves. In this context that means nurturing our own growth and self-realization. Through personal growth and self-realization, we can contribute more both to the enhancement of others' lives and to the life of the world. Florence van Straten puts it this way.

> What this means to me is that every human being is now charged with a new responsibility. The evolutionary process for us is no longer a matter of passing on "good" genes to offspring but a duty to pass on the results of our creative activities — artistic, scientific, inter-personal — to the coming generations. . . . This is where the evolutionary ladder takes on a new twist and reaches into a new dimension. This adds a new dimension to what gives our life meaning.[19]

In Julian Huxley's words, we are "the trustees of evolution." It is our responsibility to chart a better future. We are part of a Great Living System and our lives gain meaning insofar as we participate in life-enlargement and life-enrichment and oppose all that would diminish and destroy life. Some of us will be leaders and some will be followers. As far as the question of meaning is concerned, it does not matter if our contribution is large or small. What matters is not the quantity but the quality of our contribution. What matters is that we are part of the process, that we identify ourselves with those communities and movements that are aiming toward human betterment.

The second myth, or perhaps second dimension of the myth emerging today, is the unity of all things. This spatial dimension of the myth points to the interconnectedness and interdependence of all life linked together by shared resources and common needs, rooted and grounded in a common Source. This myth finds expression in one of the principles of the Unitarian Universalist Association which affirms "the interdependent web of all existence of which we are a part."

It is found in modern writers, as in the passage quoted in Chapter One from Alice Walker's *The Color Purple*. Fifty years ago John Steinbeck depicted it in *The Grapes of Wrath*. Early in the book the preacher Casey tells Tom's family of his struggle with his faith, and how, like Jesus, he went into the wilderness to sort things out.

> Nighttime I'd lay on my back an' look up at the stars; morning I'd set an' watch the sun come up; midday I'd look out from a hill at the rollin' dry country; evenin' I'd foller the sun down. Sometimes I'd pray like I'd always done. On'y I couldn't figure what I was prayin' to or for. There was the hills, an' there was me, an' we wasn't separate no more. We was one thing. An' that one thing was holy.[20]

In denying the idea of special creation, Frederick Gilkey reminds us, Darwin

> gave us a place in a family that embraces all life on earth. When I look into the eyes of a gorilla in the zoo, I don't see a dumb beast, but a cousin, a remote one, to be sure, but a genuine relative. Is it not a source of strength to see all life on this planet as profoundly, intimately, and truly related?[21]

Recent scientific discoveries reinforce this sense of oneness. George Wald notes that despite the great variety of life forms which have evolved over the millenia, the basic biological entities differ little.

> The biological cells which constitute a maple leaf, a caterpillar, and a human brain are basically the same in structure and components; the organisms have achieved different forms by organizing the cells in different patterns and calling upon them to perform different functions.[22]

Wald writes that biologists have recently become acutely aware of the kinship of all living organisms. Few changes have occurred in the structures of the proteins and genes constituting the basic building blocks of all life. Wald points out, for example, that in the remote past humans shared a common ancestor with yeast.

> From that remote ancestor, yeast went its way, and we went ours. The journey has been made twice, yet has resulted in such minor differences. So, all life is akin; and our kinship is much closer than we had ever imagined before.[23]

Even breathing exhibits our relatedness. One estimate holds that owing to the thorough mixing of the Earth's atmosphere, each of our inhalations contains at least one atom breathed by each person on Earth within the last few weeks. "That air is carried by the lungs into the bloodstream. It becomes a part of you" and that means that our breathing constitutes nothing less than "a low-frequency chain of chemical contact between all living humans and with all humans past and present." [24] It may be an exaggeration to say that each time we inhale we take in one atom exhaled by every other person, but the point that we breathe common atoms is valid. Our lives are interconnected.

In this global village of ours, we are becoming more and more aware that what happens to one person or group affects all of us. When there is oppression and violence in Central America, we suffer, too. When the Solidarity movement in Poland wins an election and seats a Prime Minister, we win, too. That lone student who dared to face a tank in Tiananmen Square did not stand alone. Millions all over the world stood with him in spirit.

Each time I buy a box of cereal in the grocery store or a gallon of gas at the service station, I know that I stand at the end of a long process to which many people have contributed. We may feel like separate and distinct individuals and we may too often act as though we are separate and distinct individuals. We are not. We are inter-dependent and interrelated.

Norman Cousins has written,

> I am a single cell in a body of four billion cells. The body is humankind. I glory in the miracle of self, but my individuality does not separate me from the oneness of humanity . . . Human unity is the fulfil-ment of diversity. It is the harmony of opposites, a many-sided texture with color and depth.[25]

Quite different from the highly individualistic perspective of liberal religion heretofore, this is an increasingly accepted perspective among Unitarian Universalists.

Earlier I quoted Albert Einstein suggesting that "the religion of the future . . . should be based on a religious sense arising from *the experience of all things as a mean-ingful unity.*" [26] More and more there are signs that such a religious sense is emerging. If it is, we may be standing at the threshold of a sea-change in the human spirit, a revolu-tion in our thinking and world view comparable to those ushered in by Moses and Copernicus. And as with the Mosaic and Copernican revolutions, it comes with enormous ethical implications, for change in our thinking must inevi-tably lead to changes in our actions. At least two ethical implications follow.

First, awareness of our unity with and dependence upon nature should lead to greater respect for the interdependent web of all existence, which in turn should lead to increased efforts to conserve our precious resources. Conservation will require us to reduce our level of consumption, which is currently gross over-consumption, to waste less and re-cycle more, and to stop filling the air and the water with pollutants.

But the sense of unity and interdependence among all human beings leads to even more basic changes. Instead of every person serving primarily himself or herself, all of us must learn to put the good of the whole community ahead of our own private welfare. *Instead of looking out for number one, we must learn to look out for one another.* We must learn to make decisions not on the basis of what is best for *me*, but what is best for *us*. We must learn cooperation instead of competition.

We cannot continue to adhere to the creed that "greed is good," for the world has shrunk and our greed and selfishness are harmful to others, as theirs is to us. We are inter-related. We must learn not only that "when I cut a tree my arm will bleed," but that when another person is gunned down by an assault rifle, my life is diminished, that when the democratic movement in China is crushed, a part of me is crushed as well.

This emerging myth of the unity and interconnectedness of all life may be understood from the perspective of either an open humanism or a natural theism. A naturalistic theist would simply add that the sense of oneness is founded upon and grounded in belief in the kind of God described in Chapter One, God the Power of Life and Love immanent in the world, God the Source of all, God the Sea of which each individual life form is but a momentary wave.

This God — understood not as a supernatural being separate from humankind and the world who relates to us as a powerful lawgiver and parent — is, rather, the creative power within all that is, or the magnetic force that energizes and pushes us toward goodness, love, beauty and truth. God is immanent, not other. Moreover, God is not complete and unchanging as in the traditional Western conception, but is also evolving and involved in the evolutionary, ongoing creation. And, God is neither omniscient nor omnipotent. God learns and grows as the universe unfolds.

Charles Hartshorne has referred to the world as "God's body," a phrase reminiscent of Alexander Pope's lines:

> All are parts of one stupendous whole
> Whose body Nature is and God the soul.[27]

When we understand our individual lives as part of one great universal process, we see that, rather than disconnected, unrelated individuals, we are each part of a greater whole, a universe of all other people and other living things as well. The meaning of our lives is not therefore so much a matter of our own individual achievement as it is a matter of how we can work together with others to contribute to the whole. Our manner of living, the decisions we make, and the actions we take play a role in the ongoing process of the Great Living System. Although our individual contribution may seem slight, it is part of the sum of all those actions which together shape the course of history.

We have come full circle. For at the outset we suggested that the modern world has lost the sense that life is meaningful because it is part of a divine grand design in which each person has a role to play. That loss of faith in a meaningful life is rooted in loss of faith in a divine being, traditionally understood. The old myths and symbols have lost their power for our age. We need a new form of conceptualization, a new mythos, a new symbolization compatible with the modern world view. The vision described above, drawing on a modern scientific world view, offers a new way of understanding our lives as meaningful in a larger context. Our lives do play a role in an ongoing divine process.

Conclusion

We are the beings who ask the question of meaning. Much of the time the question remains in our subconscious, and we are not aware of meaning as a problem. We take it as given that life is worth living. But from time to time, often when we experience grief or shock, the question intrudes, and the problem of meaning becomes crucial. When that happens a religious perspective becomes important, as does a community which lifts up a vision of what makes our lives worth living. We cannot count on a chance revelation from an unexpected source, as in the Woody Allen movie.

We have suggested a perspective on the question of meaning and purpose, a liberal religious view. But it is important to have more than a theoretical approach, a theology. Religion involves appropriation by the self and assimilation of what one believes. It also involves the continual reinforcement of one's beliefs and values. In this, the religious community plays a vital role.

Religious communities point the way to meaningful living and reinforce our belief in life's meaningfulness by means of songs, stories, myths, symbols, rituals, sermons and readings, celebrations of the passages of life, and through the love, friendship and support of others who share our lives and experiences in a meaningful way. The liberal religious community provides these kinds of support through worship services, support and growth groups, one-to-one relationships, and social service groups.

Tim, the young man who came to me seeking a reason for living, recently left his job in business and went back to school to prepare to teach math in an inner city high school. He feels that he has found the meaning and direction he had previously lacked. He is excited and very happy; for he sees his new work as a way of contributing to the enrichment of individuals and of human life as a whole. I believe it will also enable him to savor life more.

Everyone of us needs to feel a sense of meaning and purpose in living. To find and live that sense is a religious task. Within the broad context of the liberal religious perspective, there are many kinds of work and many ways to find and live a deep and satisfying sense of meaning and direction, ways in which we contribute to the ongoing universal evolutionary process of life-enlargement and enrichment.

PART III

THE CRISIS
OF
PAIN AND SUFFERING

6

WHY DO BAD THINGS HAPPEN
TO GOOD PEOPLE?

Man that is born of woman is of few days and full
of trouble.

Job 14:1

And if the sufferings of children go to swell the sum
of sufferings which was necessary to pay for truth,
then I protest that the truth is not worth such a
price.

Ivan Karamasov, The Brothers Karamasov,
by Fyodor Dostoevsky

Until my dying day I shall refuse to love a scheme
of things in which little children are put to torture.

Dr. Rieux, The Plague, by Albert Camus

The Traditional Problem of Suffering

Several years ago I received a call from a church member
asking me to see her niece whose six-year-old daughter was
dying of cancer. The young mother had no church affiliation
and wanted to talk about her daughter's imminent funeral.
The aunt thought her niece might also need help with her
feelings about her daughter's illness and impending death.

I called on the young mother the next day. We talked,
and she showed me a picture of her daughter taken before
she became ill. Her daughter was a beautiful and bright-
looking child. I was saddened to think that such a lovely
child would not be able to live a long life. I asked to see the
little girl even though she was sleeping because of the heavy
sedation given to reduce her pain. I was sickened by what I

saw. She was very thin, the left side of her face was swollen by tumors and her left eye bulged grotesquely. That once beautiful and healthy child was now an ugly disfigured skeleton of a little girl. My heart ached, and I fought unsuccessfully to hold back the tears. I could only imagine how much more pain and hurt that mother felt.

I also found myself feeling angry, angry that this could happen to such a sweet and innocent little girl. Why did this child have to suffer so horribly and die? Surely she had done nothing to deserve such a fate. Was her mother being punished because she had borne the girl unmarried? Surely not, for the punishment was far worse than the offense. What kind of a world is this anyway, in which innocent little children suffer like this and die before they have really lived?

That was not the first time I had asked those questions, although perhaps never before with so much passion. I had asked those questions many years ago when I learned about Auschwitz and Buchenwald, and again when I saw nightly televised reports from Vietnam showing women and children slaughtered, and again when I saw the shrunken bodies and swollen stomachs of starving children in Africa, and so on — too many times, too many times.

One of the major reasons I had become a religious liberal was that I had not found satisfactory answers to these questions in traditional Christianity. The age-old question of why bad things happen to good people had led to a religious crisis for me, as it has for many others. The experience of pain and suffering often leads to a personal crisis because it shatters the foundations on which we build our lives. In particular it shatters our view of the world as a just and decent and meaningful place.

Why bad things happen to good people has been a tormenting question for human beings for millenia, perhaps since the beginning of human consciousness. Religion has been asked to explain the prevalence and persistence of suffering.

One of the earliest answers to the question is the view that pain and suffering are the consequence of sin. According to this theory, God punishes people for their wicked deeds and rewards them for their good acts. This view was dominant throughout most of the Old Testament, although an occasional voice questioned it. The most powerful rejection of it came late in the Old Testament period, in the *Book of Job*. The story is familiar. Job, a wealthy, righteous, God-fearing man, loses his possessions, then his children, and finally his own health is broken. In his pain and anguish Job tries to understand why he is allowed to suffer so terribly when his evil neighbors continue to prosper and live enjoyable lives. Until these catastrophes befell him, he had accepted the traditional understanding of suffering as a punishment for one's transgressions. But Job insisted that he was a decent man. He did not deserve the awful pain inflicted upon him. Despite the counsel of his so-called comforters to repent of his sins and ask for God's mercy, Job refused. He knew he was right. He knew he did not deserve what had befallen him. The traditional answer did not square with reality, and the book of Job was written to challenge that position.

In the New Testament Jesus also repudiates the identification of suffering with punishment. When he is asked whether a certain man's blindness was caused by the man himself or by his parents, Jesus replies, "Neither this man nor his parents sinned." Human suffering, he was saying, is not the result of God's punishment for our wrong-doings.

Very few if any religious liberals believe that suffering is punishment. Yet many of us still think that way at least subconsciously; for whenever a tragic event occurs, often the first question that comes to mind is: "What did I do to deserve this?"

We tend to believe the world is just and orderly, and if that is the case, then there must be a good reason why we suffer. Hence we try to blame someone or something, and often we can think of reasons to blame ourselves. "If only I had gotten him to a doctor sooner . . ." "If only I had been there at the time . . ."

In my first parish, a couple active in the church had lost their only son at the age of fourteen in an auto accident. As I talked with them about it, it became clear that to some degree at least they felt that something they had done had been responsible for their son's death, and nothing I said could dissuade them from that view. It was as though they needed to believe their son's death was a punishment for their sins.

I now know there are both psychological and theological reasons for the persistence of the view of suffering as punishment. Psychologically it is a way of dealing with the guilt every person feels; for if suffering is a punishment for sin, then it becomes a way to atone for sin.

Theologically, the persistence of the idea that suffering is a divine punishment involves the whole concept of a just universe. If goodness is not rewarded and evil is not punished, it is difficult to maintain that we live in a just, fair, and orderly cosmos. And if the universe is not just, then what does that do to belief in God? That twentieth century

Job, Archibald MacLeish's J.B., cries out in his anguished effort to understand why he lost his children: "We have no choice but to be guilty. God is unthinkable if we are innocent." [1]

The traditional problem of suffering is usually stated something like this: If God is both perfectly good and all-powerful, as the Biblical tradition seems to maintain, how can God allow suffering and evil? For, if God is truly good, God would not permit the existence of suffering and evil, and if God is all-powerful, God would be able to prevent suffering and evil. The traditional understanding of God leads to a dilemma: God is either not all-powerful or He is not good. Neither option is acceptable to the traditional theist.

The problem of the goodness of God in the face of undeserved suffering is confronted by Ivan Karamasov in Dostoevsky's great novel, *The Brothers Karamasov*. To Ivan it might be possible to justify the suffering and death of adults, but there can be no justification for the suffering of innocent children. At one point in the novel Ivan relates several incidents of brutality perpetrated on little children, and he expresses his outrage at a God who allows such unjust suffering. "I must have justice, . . . not justice in some remote infinite time and space, but here on earth, and that I could see myself." [2] It is not so much that Ivan doubts God's existence, but that he repudiates a God who is unjust. If the sufferings of little children are necessary to pay for the harmony of the world or to pay for truth, then for Ivan the price is too high. Ivan cannot love a God who allows children to be tortured nor can he love a world in which innocent children suffer.

This is also the theme of Albert Camus' novel *The Plague* in which the twentieth-century city of Oran is struck by bubonic plague. One of the principal characters is a priest who at first maintains that the people were suffering and dying because God is punishing them for their sins and calling them to repentance. After working with the dying, the priest's position softens, and in his next sermon dealing with the problem he confesses that he does not understand but believes that we must trust and love what we cannot understand. He also says that the Christian must suffer and sacrifice herself or himself as Christ suffered and gave himself.

The principal character in the book, however, is not the priest but a physician, Dr. Rieux. After Rieux and the priest have worked side by side in a vain effort to save a dying child, they engage in a brief conversation. The priest expresses sad acceptance of the child's death, but Dr. Rieux is angry. "Perhaps we should love what we cannot understand," says the priest, reiterating the theme of his second sermon. "No, Father," replies Dr. Rieux, reminiscent of Ivan Karamasov, "I've a very different idea of love. And until my dying day I shall refuse to love a scheme of things in which little children are put to torture." [3]

Ivan's and Dr. Rieux's outrage at the apparent injustice of the universe is the modern version of Job's protest. The difference lies in the answers given to the problem of suffering. Near the end of the *Book of Job* God finally answers out of the whirlwind:

> Where were you when I laid the foundation of the earth? Tell me, if you have understanding.
> Who determined its measurements — surely you know!
> Have you commanded the morning since your days

began.. Can you bind the chains of the Pleaides? ..."

(from Chapter 38)

God's words may be interpreted as a severe reprimand. "Who are you to question my ways and judge my wisdom? I am God and you are but a man. Trust me and keep your place; don't try to comprehend that which is for you incomprehensible. Don't question my purposes." And Job gets the message. He repents and acknowledges that it was presumptuous of him to think that he should understand the deepest mysteries of life. His role was simply to trust that the Omnipotent was wise and good.

There is wisdom in that point of view and there is comfort and consolation. But for Ivan and Dr. Rieux and for many of the liberally religious, it is neither intellectually satisfying nor morally adequate.

The Biblical tradition offers other explanations of suffering than the idea of punishment. One is the notion that suffering is a test of faith. In the *Prologue* to the *Book of Job*, Satan persuades God to inflict suffering on Job as a test of his faithfulness. Today, too, we sometimes hear people justifying pain or suffering by regarding it as a test of their commitment to God or his cause. One may wonder, however, what kind of God puts people to such tests as incurable cancer or the death of a child. The notion of suffering as a deliberate test of faith initiated by God raises as many questions about God's goodness and justice as it purports to answer.

Another view is that evil and suffering are the work of God's archenemy, the Devil. But that, too, raises more questions than it answers. For, if God created Satan, then God is still ultimately responsible for evil and suffering. And if the Devil was not created by God, then he is a second god, an evil god, and God is not all-powerful. We are back to the original dilemma. God is either not good or not omnipotent.

One of the more prevalent justifications of suffering is the view that the balance will be put right after death. If there is injustice in this life, it will be corrected in the next life when the good will be rewarded and the evil punished. This is one of the views associated with Christianity. The great eighteenth-century philosopher Immanuel Kant, often called the most Protestant of philosophers, held it. For Kant it was clear that goodness was not always rewarded, and evil was not always punished. However, Kant could not believe in a capricious universe or a God who acted less than justly. So he maintained that the injustices of this life would be rectified in the next. So strong was his belief in ultimate justice as a philosophical necessity that he saw it as a kind of proof of immortality. But if one cannot believe in a life after death in which the scales will be balanced, this view fails to satisfy.

Also central to the Christian tradition is the belief that suffering can be redemptive. If one has sinned, perhaps by suffering one can be relieved of guilt and feel that one has atoned for his or her wrongdoing. This idea is extended in the concept of vicarious suffering. Christ's suffering on the cross is believed to atone for the sins of others and thus to redeem them. Deep in the Christian tradition is the view that the suffering of believers may help to transform their lives and the lives of others.

Soren Kierkegaard writes out of this conviction when he says that the way of purification is affliction. He also believed that suffering was essential to achievement and that there is joy in suffering when you know that suffering is the right way.

These, then, represent the major traditional attempts to answer the questions of why there is suffering and evil at all, and in particular of why bad things happen to good people. Most religious liberals do not find them satisfying, in some cases because we are operating out of a different philosophical/theological framework and in other cases because, like Ivan Karamasov and Dr. Rieux, they offend our sense of justice. In fact many of us were driven, as I was, from traditional to liberal religion precisely because we could not reconcile the prevalence of suffering and evil with the traditional concept of God. We turn now to some liberal approaches to the problem of pain and suffering.

Liberal Approaches to Pain and Suffering

The first question we must ask is whether the question, "why bad things happen to good people," poses an intellectual or theological problem for the liberally religious in the way it does for the more traditionally religious. Since liberal religion includes both theistic and humanistic perspectives, we must look at the answers each perspective offers.

For the humanist, it is not necessary to try to reconcile the concept of a good and all-powerful God with the existence of suffering. The traditional problem of theodicy simply does not exist in the familiar way. If, however, the humanist has no need to justify the ways of God, he or she does need to maintain a faith that life is good and worth living despite the existence of pain and suffering, despite the fact that innocent people suffer and die prematurely. Therefore, it is still important to understand why bad things happen to good people.

From both perspectives human freedom will be seen as one of the causes of suffering. Some of the choices we make bring suffering. If I drink too much and then drive my car, have an accident and severely injure myself, I have suffered as a result of my own poor choices. I can also inflict mental suffering on myself by, for example, castigating myself for an unwise decision I made years ago. I will suffer as a result of my own poor judgment.

The choices we make not only affect ourselves but often affect others too, and the choices others make sometimes affect us. Someone who drives while intoxicated may have an accident and injure or kill others. Something I say or fail to say may hurt another person. The unspeakable horrors of Nazism and of Stalinism were all the result of choices made by one person or group of people. There are countless instances in which we human beings acting alone or in concert inflict pain and suffering on one another. Because we are to some extent free, we are also free to inflict great hurt and suffering on our fellow human beings.

Freedom is the source of our greatest triumphs. Indeed, we would be less than human without freedom. But it is one of life's paradoxes that this gift of freedom is the source of both our grandeur and also our misery. There is a correlation between our capacity for self-determination and for good and evil. The greater our capacity for self-determination, the greater is our capacity for good or evil. The nature of things is such that these go together. Yet most religious liberals hold that one of the goals of human life is to increase the degree of our self-determination, our freedom, though, ironically, that also means we increase our capacity to cause pain and suffering.

Another reason bad things happen is the inhumanity of human beings to one another. Liberal religion has in the past been reluctant to speak of sin and evil. This is a weakness that comes of our history. Liberal religion in America was born in reaction to the orthodox emphasis on original sin and human depravity. Liberals held that human beings did not come into the world with a predisposition toward evil, as these dogmas insisted. Liberals held — and hold — that we are born good and educable, and the way we are treated socially plays an important role in the degree to which we lead constructive or destructive lives.

But we can recognize the extent of human malice and perversity without the dogma of original sin. From modern psychology we have learned of the potential for evil within the shadowy depths of the psyche. From evolutionary biology we have learned of the centrality of the instinct for self-preservation, which is easily transmuted into self-centeredness. We know that when our self-interests collide with the interests of others, we tend to pursue our own interests. Sometimes this leads to suffering on the part of another. When as part of a divorce settlement, for example, two people fight over shared property or the custody of their children, the one who loses suffers a great deal as do the children. The self-interests of two people are in conflict.

Moreover, self-centeredness can become exaggerated or perverted and lead to cruelty. This happens, for example, when one person feels that another stands in his way, and he inflicts injury to get him out of the way. Even the best of us do not always will the good of others.

Sometimes when our self-interests seem threatened, we develop an animosity far out of proportion to our needs, and we may inflict injury far beyond that necessary for self-protection. An escalating animosity like that may have been at work in the long history of anti-Semitism which led to the atrocities of the Nazis against the Jews. Those atrocities can only be understood as the expression of human malice, vindictiveness, and bigotry. Those and other events of the twentieth century have forced religious liberals to reconsider our conception of human nature and to develop a modern doctrine of evil.

Ironically, even good intentions and lofty ideals may be transmuted into evil that causes suffering. I may steadfastly pursue what I believe are basically good goals, but in doing so trample on others in such a way as to cause them suffering. For example I may push others aside as I seek professional advancement, or in trying to help others I may reinforce a dependency that harms them. In his excellent book, *The Devil and Dr. Church*, Forrest Church shows how such virtues as tolerance, respectability, knowledge, sophistication and piety can be perverted into evil.[4]

Unwavering devotion to the essentially good goals of one's country or ideology or organization can lead to suffering. The American involvement in Vietnam illustrates this. We went into Vietnam out of good intentions, to save the country from communism. So convinced were we that our cause was just that we lost perspective and brought great suffering to many people.

When we believe we are right, we must be especially careful lest that rightness become self-righteousness which carries with it a sense of superiority over others and belief that we may impose our way on them for their own good. Good people and basically good nations or groups can bring evil and suffering on themselves and others unintentionally when that happens.

Thoughtlessness, carelessness, self-centeredness, pride, greed, envy — all these and many other "natural" human traits are often at the base of actions we do or fail to do that bring suffering to other people.

Both theistic and humanistic liberals can accept the fact that we humans bring a good deal of suffering upon ourselves. From a theistic perspective this point is made in a humorous way in the movie *Oh, God!* God, played by George Burns, defends himself against the charge that he is responsible for evil by saying, "I did not create the evil; I gave you humans a perfectly good world, but *you* messed it up!"

More broadly, bad things happen to good people because of the interrelatedness of life. Each life is dependent on others for its very existence, its nourishment, for example. We humans feed upon vegetable and animal life; some forms of life feed upon us. The flu virus which recently afflicted me was simply feeding on me as I feed on other forms of life. It was fulfilling its innate need to grow and develop or at least to survive, but in the process it made me suffer.

Life is interrelated. Events that transpire anywhere on our planet may bring suffering upon *us*, just as they may also bring benefits. An assassination, a coup d'état, a hostile act by one nation against another anywhere in our global village may have adverse repercussions elsewhere.

Much of our suffering is caused by nature, sometimes by what we call "natural disasters" and at other times simply by the operation of the laws of nature. To the liberally religious, natural forces that harm humans need not be understood as dispensed by the will of God. There need be no intentionality involved; these things just happen. An earthquake that takes the lives of hundreds of people and inflicts great pain on countless others is simply the result of geological movements. It is by chance alone that it occurred in Lisbon or San Francisco. Many more earthquakes occur where no humans are involved, at the bottom of the ocean, for example.

Again, the operation of the laws of nature may sometimes cause pain and suffering and death to humans. If a person is killed by a falling rock, that is because the rock was obeying the law of gravity. A plane that loses power on takeoff and plummets to earth, killing scores of people, is obeying the law of gravity. For the most part, gravity is our benefactor. Without it, there would be no planet earth or life as we know it. Yet gravity can be the indirect cause of suffering.

And still again, as Peter Fleck notes, some of our suffering is inherent in the human condition. "There will always be unfulfilled hopes, frustrated aspirations, shattered love, the loss of parents, children, and friends, sickness, and ultimate death." [5] To be human is to suffer physically and mentally; we cannot escape it.

We are all part of a great living system. We are not exempt from its laws, and sometimes its operations and interactions can result in pain and suffering for one or more of us. That is simply another, a modern, demythologized way of saying what the *Book of Job* counsels. God admonished Job for looking at his situation solely from a self-centered point of view, suggesting that he look at things from a larger, a cosmic perspective. When we look at life and the world *sub specie aeternitatis*, from a perspective that is not human-centered, the question of why we suffer seems rather small up against the vast mystery of existence.

Because liberal theology does not need to find a purpose in everything that happens, we can recognize the possibility

of random occurrences. The world is both orderly and cha-
otic. Some things happen as a result of order in the universe,
but other things occur haphazardly. Knowing that some
things happen without a reason makes it easier to accept
them than it would be if we believed all miseries are part of
God's design.

Knowing that can be a source of comfort as is illustrated
by this eloquent testimony I received from a church member:

> Our older daughter, her husband, and their two
> infant daughters died in a fire in their home
> [several] years ago. If I thought for one moment
> that this were somehow part of a universal design,
> or ultimate reality, or God's purpose, I not only
> would reject God, I would seek to destroy anything
> so merciless, so wicked. Fortunately, my Unitarian
> understanding has taught me that part of life is
> haphazard, senseless, coincidental. Our loss is just as
> great, but the sorrow, the tragedy, becomes bear-
> able.[6]

A few years ago a young woman in my congregation was
diagnosed as having terminal cancer. While undergoing che-
motherapy, she received a letter from a fundamentalist minister who said the cancer was clearly God's punishment of
her for her sins. Understandably upset and angry, she
showed me the letter and asked me why I thought she had
been afflicted. After telling her how cruel and unchristian I
thought the letter was, I assured her that her cancer was not
God's punishment. We tried to find something in her background that might account for her cancer. That her mother
had died of cancer as a young woman seemed to suggest a
genetic tendency, and we concluded that her illness was
simply a case of bad genes. It was purely by chance that she
and her mother had inherited a propensity toward that kind

of cancer. It was a case of bad luck, not of being a bad person.

On January 13, 1982, I boarded a plane at Washington National Airport to fly to my mother's funeral. It was snowing hard, and I had some real misgivings about flying in such weather. But I wanted, and needed, to be in Missouri. My plane did not fly that day. Just a few minutes before we were to take off, Air Florida flight 90 crashed into the Potomac River, killing all but five of those on board. It could have been my plane that crashed. That it was not is to some extent a matter of chance. I do not believe I was spared while others died because I deserved to live and they did not. Their plane and not mine had a pilot inexperienced in bad weather flying. Perhaps it was also simply chance that the cancer virus took hold and grew in the body of that lovely little six-year-old girl whom I mentioned earlier.

That some suffering is due to circumstances over which we have no control can be consoling. If, for example, we know that schizophrenia and alcoholism are genetically based, it is comforting to know it was not the nature of our parenting that caused our child to be schizophrenic or to become alcoholic. There are things for which someone is responsible, and it is important to recognize real responsibility. But it is also true that there are things for which no one is responsible. It is important to recognize that too and to know the difference so that we can do something about those things which we can control.

Pain and suffering occur because of thoughtless, irresponsible, malicious, selfish or immature actions of ourselves or others, some of which are intentional and some of which are unintentional, because of the normal operations of nature, and because of the interrelatedness of all things. There is not a plan or purpose for everything that happens; some events occur randomly.

Liberal religious theists can agree with many of these assertions, since a theist need not see God as using divine power to interfere with either the laws of nature or human freedom. From the perspective of naturalistic theism God is the Creative Power or Life Force within humankind and within all of life that pushes or pulls life and the world toward health, growth, love and unity. That creative force is identified as *good*, but not necessarily as *omnipotent*. It is understood as engaging with us and empowering us in the struggle to overcome the forces within life which cause pain and suffering and evil and premature death, but it is not understood as all-powerful in the manner of traditional theism.

Modern process theology, based on the philosophy of Alfred North Whitehead, provides a metaphysical framework for such a conception of God. Uniting a theistic world view with a modern scientific understanding of the universe, it offers a helpful perspective on the problem of suffering by suggesting, first, that God is good but not all-powerful. God is not in complete control of the world, and therefore cannot be blamed for inflicting pain and suffering. Not power but love is the primary attribute of God. God's power is the power of love. God does not exercise power in a coercive or controlling way. Rather, God's power is the magnetic power of persuasion.

God has certain goals for the world which God seeks to accomplish by persuading human beings to act according to these goals, but God does not or cannot force people to do what God wants or what is best for them. This insight is in harmony with the understanding that if we humans truly love another, we will not try to control that person. God's love is similar to our own in that regard. This view retains the reality of human freedom, since in freedom human beings can refuse to conform to the divine aims for human life. We may choose evil and in so doing cause pain and suffering. Therefore, "since God is not in complete control of the events of the world, the occurrence of genuine evil is not incompatible with God's beneficence toward all his creatures." [7]

For process theology, God is limited by the nature of things. God is limited by human freedom with its possibilities for choices that may bring suffering. God is limited by the conflict of human wills that leads to suffering for some. And God is limited by a natural world in which random events may affect human beings adversely.

The divine Creative Force is not something separate and distinct from life and the world, which wills whatever happens. The image of God, drawn from the infant's relationship with its seemingly omnipotent parents, must be revised, as children revise the image of their parents when they learn that their parents are not responsible for everything that happens. The Creative Force may be understood as the power constantly at work within life and the world for goodness, truth, wholeness and beauty. Such a God does not interfere with human freedom or the functioning of the natural world.

Further, process theology also holds that God enters into and is affected by human suffering. God is present in the life forces within the body as it struggles against disease. God shares the pain, assisting the person to find serenity and acceptance even in the face of death. God is also present in the love and care given by others and in the dedicated efforts of medical scientists to find cures for illness.

What about the suffering caused, not by human error or malice, but by such natural occurrences as earthquakes and tornadoes and viral infections? According to process theology, we live in an imperfect and unfinished universe. Creation is not a once-for-all event but an ongoing, perhaps never-ending, process, and we are a part of it.

We cannot stop earthquakes and tornadoes, but we can and do take measures to reduce the harm they can cause. By learning to predict them, we can warn people to leave the areas about to be hit. By learning to construct stronger buildings in dangerous areas, we can mitigate the destructive force of natural disasters. Similarly, medical scientists can and do develop methods to fight bacteria and viruses so that suffering can be reduced. Smallpox, measles, and polio are three serious diseases which have been virtually eliminated by vaccines. Perhaps cancer or AIDS will be next.

Involvement in scientific and cultural advances which help to alleviate pain and suffering not only enables us to participate in the ongoing creation, but at the same time gives meaning and purpose to our lives. Ironically, the very realities that bring pain and suffering also provide opportunities for making life more meaningful and worth living.

Thus, process theology offers a twofold answer to the question of why good people suffer. Anthony Friess Perrino says it well.

> God wanted his children to grow — so he gave them freedom, and he wanted their lives to have meaning — so he gave them an unfinished world with the opportunity to share in its creation.[8]

In contrast to traditional theology, a liberal theology, whether theist or humanist, offers answers to the problem of suffering which are both intellectually and morally satisfying.

However, the intellectual realm is but one aspect of the crisis of pain and suffering. The other aspect is personal. How are we to cope with pain and suffering when they strike? The next chapter will deal with the resources liberal religion offers us when that happens.

7

RESPONDING CREATIVELY
TO PAIN AND SUFFERING

When did we ever learn that life was always
    Summertime and Spring and harvest time?
When was it that someone guaranteed a year
    of twelve Julys,
complete with everlasting picnics and
    never-ending potato salads?
What sort of quaint, mistaken almanac said
    Spring could come without December —
That life was all in June —
    That May and August go on forever?
Even Winter in ourselves may be the poor
    soul's fertilizer,
And Spring within can come only if some
    Winter has come first —
Can come, if something like a seed is kept
    alive through wintering, to sprout and grow.
Like earth, we have our seasons too.

           Max Coots, *Seasons of the Self*

All sunshine makes a desert.

           Arab saying

Suffering produces endurance, and endurance produces character and character produces hope.

           Romans 5:3-4

Suffering makes men [sic] think, thinking makes
them wise, and wisdom makes the world endurable.

        The Teahouse of the August Moon

It is important to thinking people to understand why we
suffer. However, the greatest problem suffering brings for
many of us is not theoretical, but practical, how to endure

pain and suffering and somehow live well in spite of them. For the liberally religious it is a matter of maintaining faith that life is good and worth living in the midst of deep suffering or loss. Viktor Frankl writes that "suffering ceases to be suffering in some way at the moment it finds a meaning," [9] and he quotes Nietzsche: "He who has a *why* to live for can bear with almost any *how*." [10]

The first step on the way to living well in the midst of suffering involves accepting suffering as an integral part of life. To accept suffering is not to encourage it or to imply that we must like it, but to recognize it as a normal and natural aspect of life, a part of life without which human life would be very different from what we know. To accept suffering is to accept the reality that life includes both tragedy and joy. It is also to see suffering as an opportunity for growth and maturation.

In the Buddhist tradition there is a story of a young mother who brings her dead baby to the Buddha, asking for a miraculous resurrection. The Buddha neither grants nor denies her request but simply directs the woman first to find one household that has not been touched by sorrow. Every one to whom she talks has a story to tell about pain or sorrow or anguish, and so when the woman returns from her journey she withdraws her request. Seeing the prevalence of sorrow had helped her to accept her own.

It may seem obvious that since suffering exists, we must learn to accept it. But we live in and are deeply influenced by a society that does not like to face up to unpleasantness of any kind. We put all our efforts into eliminating pain through medication, and we seldom address the issue of how to deal creatively with suffering.

Several years ago I became seriously ill and required hospitalization. While I was ill, I became acutely aware of how great a blessing good health is. As I was recovering, I clearly remember feeling a heightened consciousness of how wonderful life is and how much I enjoyed even the simplest everyday things. I also resolved that when I got well, I would make the most of every day and every experience. Someone has said, "Happiness exists by the grace of a certain amount of unhappiness." The experience of many people corroborates mine. It sometimes takes pain and suffering to enable us to appreciate the joy and richness that is ours just by virtue of being alive. Max Coots put it well.

> Winter in ourselves may be the poor soul's fertilizer,
> And Spring within can come only if some
> Winter has come first.[11]

Suffering can force us to plumb the depths of our experience and thus enhance our lives and also, then, the contribution we make to the world. Most of us know of people whose lives have been transformed as a result of serious illness or emotional anguish. While in college, my oldest son suffered a potentially life-threatening illness which caused him to reexamine his values and the direction his life was taking. Feeling that up to that point he had lived only for himself and had done nothing to help others, he decided to take a year off from school to work for subsistence wages rehabilitating houses for a non-profit group that then sold those houses to low-income people at cost.

One measure of our lives is the quality of our response in the face of pain and suffering. Our response determines whether suffering has a positive or a negative meaning. The crucial question regarding suffering is not "Why did this happen?" Rather it is, "What can I do about it?" or "How can I make this meaningful?"

Many examples come to mind of people who have converted suffering or loss into a positive experience. I think of Candy Lightner, whose daughter was killed by a drunk driver. Instead of spending her life mourning or feeling sorry for herself, Mrs. Lightner acted. She founded "Mothers Against Drunk Driving," a national movement against drinking and driving.

Several years ago one of the members of the church I serve was diagnosed as having colon cancer. After conferring with doctors and researching various treatments, he decided to participate in an experimental treatment having a very high remission rate although it was too early for conclusive results. By participating in this program, whether his cancer was arrested or not, his illness and treatment would contribute to medical advancement and hence to the benefit of others in the future. His suffering would have a meaning.

Suffering does not magically or automatically lead to growth or to human betterment. It can also lead to bitterness, discouragement and defeat. Yet it does seem suffering is often essential to deepen our lives and broaden our sympathies. Without our own suffering would we develop compassion and empathy for others when they suffer? Without suffering and the prospect of death would we make any effort to come to grips with the most basic human questions? It does seem that suffering can help us live more deeply and more responsibly, and it is sometimes the case that the experience of suffering is the catalyst for a positive life-change. This whole point was summarized succinctly by Dr. Harry Emerson Fosdick. A little boy one day asked him why it was that God put all the vitamins in spinach and not in ice cream. Dr. Fosdick replied that he did not know why but that life is just that way.

Having said that we learn from suffering, however, I say again, such learning is not automatic. Suffering can also embitter or defeat us. And sometimes the price is too high. What could we possibly learn that would be worth the death of a child? To be made a quadriplegic by an accident is too high a price to pay to learn that we ought to be more careful, or to learn any other lesson. I do not believe God causes such things to happen to teach us lessons we might not otherwise learn. I do not believe we suffer for any purpose of God, as the traditional theist maintains. I do believe that sometimes our suffering may be turned to good purposes. It is a matter of human will, and perhaps grace, but it is largely up to us. As Unitarian Universalist minister Tom Owen-Towle says, "We are broken people, you and I. What matters somehow is whether we become weak or strong at the broken places."

But some suffering is only destructive and without redeeming qualities. I think again of the Nazi genocide, of the sufferings of the people of Southeast Asia, of parents who lose children. Sometimes suffering is senseless and without benefit to anyone. Sometimes the benefits are tragically disproportionate to what is endured. William F. Schulz writes,

> Too much suffering can level a human being. It is not for nothing that people erect defenses, choose shallowness, and treasure good, stiff drinks. "Profound suffering makes noble," Nietzsche said. But it also shatters nerves and, much as I revere him, Nietzsche did die mad.[12]

Is life just and fair? Do we suffer to the extent that we deserve to suffer? Are we rewarded with happiness and success insofar as we deserve them? The answer of course is no. Life is not perfectly just or always fair. Much happens that is unjust and unfair. Bad things happen to good people, and good things happen to bad people. By no stretch of the imagination can the Nazi gas chambers or the Soviet gulag be said to have any part in justice. Ivan Karamasov and Dr. Rieux were right. The world is not just and life is not fair so long as little children — and a lot of other innocent people — suffer and die.

Archibald MacLeish wrestled brilliantly with this question of justice in his beautiful modern adaptation of *Job*, his play *J.B.* In many ways he follows the ancient story. J.B. is a very wealthy man with a wife whom he loves and children of whom he is justly proud. He is duly grateful to God for his many blessings. However, as in the Biblical story, one by one his children are killed, he loses all his wealth, his skin is covered with painful sores, and finally his wife leaves him because he will not defend himself. The play takes on a distinctly modern face as MacLeish makes J.B.'s "comforters" speak in terms of three principal philosophies of our time, Marxism, psychoanalysis, and conventional Christianity. Each explains J.B.'s plight from his own perspective. The Marxist proclaims that one person's suffering is inconsequential in the light of History, but J.B. repudiates that idea, insisting that the individual matters. The psychoanalyst maintains that guilt is an illusion stemming from the false idea that we think we are free to make choices. J.B. rejects this too, because to him we are less than human if we are only victims of our instincts. The preacher expounds the unhelpful idea of original sin, that humankind was created evil. J.B. finds that most repugnant because it makes God responsible for evil.

Then God speaks to J.B. using the words from the *Book of Job*. Like Job, J.B. is humbled and repents of his pride in questioning God and forgives God for the injustices he has suffered.

But that is not all. In the final scene Sarah, J.B.'s wife, returns. Her words offer a new perspective. "You wanted justice," she says to J.B., "and there was none — only love." And J.B. replies, referring to God, "He does not love. He is." "But we do," says Sarah, "and that's the wonder." [13]

Writing in this most violent of centuries, with the horrors of the second World War in the background, MacLeish is saying that there is no justice in this world. Nor can we expect to find justice in the universe. The universe does not judge; nor does it mete out rewards and punishments; it simply is. The only justice we will find is the justice we create. The answer to the problem of unjust suffering is not to be found by questioning God or the cosmos; the answer is our love, love of life, love of the world in spite of its lack of justice, and the love we can give to one another.

> Then blow on the coal of the heart, my darling
> . . . [it is Sarah speaking].
> It's all the light now.
> Blow on the coal of the heart.
> The candles in churches are out.
> The lights have gone out in the sky.
> Blow on the coal of the heart
> And we'll see by and by . . .[14]

The answer to the problem of suffering is not to be found in traditional religion or in the creation of a brilliant new metaphysical system that explains why we suffer. The answer is to be found in human warmth and compassion and caring, in our love for one another, a love that includes responsible action on behalf of others and a love of the world.

When we experience deep pain and suffering, there is no substitute for the caring presence of friends and family members. It is comforting to know that others care enough for us to be with us and to share our burden. Before my hospitalization I had often wondered whether the calls I made as a minister on members who were ill were really helpful or just intrusive. But the visits I received, the cards and phone calls and other remembrances helped me to know that I was loved and appreciated and that my return to health was important to others.

The very word religion comes from a Latin word meaning "to bind together." Religion at its best creates strong bonds between people, and those bonds need to be felt and strengthened at times of crisis. The great sociologist Emile Durkheim suggested that the primary purpose of religion in its earliest period was not to "put people in touch with God, but to put them in touch with one another." [15] The religion that does not put people in touch with one another is not a healthy and mature religion.

Sometimes the most we can do is simply to be present and to listen. I think some of the most important hospital calls I have made have been those in which I did not say much. I was simply there. Maybe I held someone's hand. To feel alone and abandoned when we are suffering adds immensely to our suffering. The care and support and encouragement of others can assist the healing process and increase the chances that the sufferer may heal and grow spiritually as well.

> Blow on the coal of the heart and we'll know
> . . . We'll know . . .

The caring community, the presence of loving friends is a very important resource offered to us by liberal religion when we experience pain and suffering. So also is the liberal religious perspective on life, on the nature and meaning of human life and of human relationships.

Our belief in the dignity and worth of each person and our faith in the potentialities of each person are important resources to the sufferer. Sometimes suffering reduces our feeling of value and worth, especially if we are incapacitated for quite a while and unable to engage in our usual meaning-giving activities. Able to draw, though, on a deep and long-held faith in our own worth and human potential, we are sustained and comforted. Such a faith can enable us to tap our inner reservoir of power, to endure pain and suffering, and possibly to make it a constructive experience.

Our faith in the sacredness of each person has a bearing on those who would minister to the suffering. For it means that each person's pain must be taken seriously because the person who is ill or grieving or dying is still a person of great worth, not to be neglected.

Our deeply held trust that life is good and worth living can sustain us in the face of adversity and inspire us to find meaning and value even in the darkest moments. It can also help us to keep from becoming bitter or sour as a result of adversity.

A member of a church I once served exemplified this attitude as well as anyone I have ever known. When I met her she had been battling cancer for several years. She was aware that her chances of living much longer were slim. Yet she did not lose hope until the last few weeks of her life, when hope was replaced by a serene acceptance. She kept her sense that life was good and that her work was important.

Liberal religion's emphasis on freedom and responsibility is important in dealing with the prevention of suffering in those cases where a wise decision can prevent suffering. We can choose, for example, not to have an affair that might wreck our marriage and family life. Or, we can act in our freedom to reduce the suffering of homeless people by working together to establish low cost housing.

Our liberal emphasis on reason and the scientific method suggests that we value and support research in both social science and medicine, research aimed at reducing suffering. The importance of medical research in this respect is obvious. Advancement in the social sciences should increase our knowledge of human behavior and its consequences so that we can better understand why we do what we do. If we can increase our understanding of the cause of evil actions, perhaps we can reduce behavior that leads to suffering.

Finally, our "commitment to justice, equity and compassion" [17] directly addresses one of the major causes of suffering in the world. When I wrote earlier that an attitude of acceptance toward suffering is important, I was not thinking of the suffering caused by unjust social systems. The moral response to injustice is outrage and opposition, what Camus called revolt. Like Dr. Rieux we need to roll up our sleeves and give ourselves unsparingly to those in need. Sometimes that may take the form of charity — giving time, food, counsel, money, etc.— to help the poor and hungry and homeless and deprived. In other circumstances it means working to change unjust social structures at the root of much suffering, structures such as racist and sexist policies which perpetuate economic inequalities.

The final answer to the problem of suffering is ethical action to change conditions that cause people to suffer. Not all suffering can be abolished. Some suffering is inherent in the human condition; we are bound by the limits of birth and death; all that we love is limited and transient. But some suffering can be alleviated by social action.

In the last chapter I wrote of Ivan Karamasov's powerful rejection of the God of a universe in which innocent children suffer and die. But Ivan's rebellion is not Dostoevsky's last word about suffering. One of the other brothers, Dmitri, is accused of killing his father. While he is on trial, he has a dream in which he is riding through the steppes of central Russia. It is winter, very cold and snowing, and he comes to a peasant village in which many of the huts have been burned down. He sees women and children who are terribly thin and wan. One woman has a baby who is desperately hungry and crying. But the woman's breasts are dry and there is no food. Dmitri asks why the babe is weeping. His driver replies that it is because they are poor and cold and have nothing to eat. And Dmitri, the self-centered, fun-loving, hard-drinking profligate who had heretofore thought of nothing but his own desires, feels

> a passion of pity, such as he had never known before . . . rising in his heart, and he wanted to cry, . . . he wanted to do something for them all, so that the babe should weep no more, so that the dark-faced, dried-up mother should not weep, that no one should shed tears again from that moment.

When he awakens from his dream, Dmitri announces, "'I've had a good dream, gentlemen.'" "This," Dostoevsky writes, "he said in a strange voice, with a new light, as of joy, in his face." [18]

If Ivan's response to the suffering of children had been to reject the world and its creator, Dmitri's is to find a new meaning and purpose to his life, a meaning centered in love and responsibility and service.

Suffering has the power to transform and to redeem. To say so is neither to justify suffering nor to detract from its pain. It is simply to acknowledge that if to be human is to suffer, so also to be human is to be subject to the possibility of growth and transformation which may be born of pain and suffering.

Christian theologian Dorothy Soelle sums it up well when she writes: "Suffering makes one more sensitive to the pain in the world. It can teach us to put forth a greater love for everything that exists." [19]

PART IV

THE CRISIS
OF
LOSS AND GRIEF

8

THE HOUR
OF LEAD

This is the Hour of Lead —
Remembered, if outlived,
As Freezing persons recollect the Snow —
First — Chill — then Stupor — then the letting
go —

Emily Dickinson

Blessed are they who mourn, for they shall be
comforted.

The Gospel of Matthew

Deep sorrow is . . . a prelude to redemption.

Abraham Heschel

H. R. was in his early eighties but vigorous and apparently in good health when his wife of fifty years died afer a long struggle with cancer. Like most marriages theirs had known some difficult times, but they had been deeply devoted to each other especially during the last fifteen or twenty years. H.R. had cared for his wife during her long illness, and after her death he missed her very much. I had many long conversations with him during which he poured out his grief. He was depressed; he felt that he had no reason to keep on living; he was lonely; he had little energy and little interest in anything; his life was empty. He tried to resume some of the activities he had enjoyed before his wife became ill — meetings at the church, contacts with friends. His son in another city invited him for an extended visit, but he did not feel well enough to accept the invitation. Nothing worked. His doctor suggested that he go into the hospital for tests to try to determine what was wrong. He did, but they found nothing. Shortly thereafter he died suddenly of a heart attack. The attending physician wrote that his heart ruptured. He died literally of a broken heart five months after his wife had died.

H. R. was my father. For five months he suffered from acute grief as a result of the loss of my mother. His grief was complicated by his age and by the fact that for the year-and-a-half of my mother's illness, Dad's life was centered entirely on her. He took her to the doctor or the hospital for treatments, he made her feel as comfortable as possible at home, waited on her, and hoped and prayed for her recovery. Except for its extremity, however, his grief is not atypical. We all experience those same feelings of sadness, depression, loneliness, emptiness, despair and many other emotions when we have suffered a great loss.

The loss can be of someone close, or of something else. We experience other kinds of losses more frequently than death, but since we mostly associate grief with death we don't usually think of other losses as a source of grief. But they are.

We know loss when we move to a different city or a different neighborhood and lose friends, familiar surroundings, groups and institutions to which we have been attached.

We know loss when we change jobs, even when the change is a promotion, because we may miss our friends and attachments from the old job.

We know loss when we lose a job or when we retire. In both instances one day you are busy and active and making a contribution as part of the work force, and you are with productive people, and the next day you no longer have a meaningful job, and you have lost contact with your friends from the workplace.

We know losses as we grow older, the loss of energy, of memory, of our ability to do certain things we once did, of some of the hopes and dreams and expectations we once had.

We know loss as our children go off on their own; or as young adults we know loss when we leave home to go to college or take a job.

We know loss when we lose a part of our body through surgery such as a mastectomy or colostomy or when we become paralyzed as a result of an accident.

We know financial loss and perhaps the loss of a sense of financial security through a bad business deal or an unwise investment or the collapse of the stock market.

Many of us know the loss of a spouse through divorce, and with that the loss of the friends we had as a couple, sometimes the loss of a house and other property, and perhaps the loss of time with our children. We may know the loss of financial security, and of a lifestyle made possible by some degree of affluence. This certainly is true for many women after a divorce. One reason divorce is so traumatic is that it involves multiple losses.

Our list could go on. The important point is that any loss can trigger the emotions we call grief. When we experience loss we tend to go through a particular process, one documented by studies of people experiencing loss. The phases of this process describe the course of grief in response to all types of loss, but the more acute the loss, the more deeply we will experience each phase. We will usually feel the loss of a person more deeply than we do the loss of other things. But "any form of loss is at root experienced as a loss of a part of the self. A portion of the very fabric of our existence is ripped." [1]

There is really no way to avoid loss, as Judith Viorst has made clear in her excellent book *Necessary Losses.*[2] The experience of loss is part of being human. The only way we can avoid loss is to avoid attachments, but to do that is to avoid life, or at least a truly human life. The person who eschews close friendships, who never lets herself care deeply about another, may succeed in avoiding the pain of parting and loss. But such a person also misses out on some of the deepest joys of life.

To be human is to know loss, and, indeed, the more fully human we are, the more loss we will know and the deeper we will feel the losses; for the more we love and care, the more we have to lose. All the things to which we become attached are transient; they pass; they decay; they die. And when we lose someone or something we love, our response is grief.

Grief is so very difficult to handle because it is not one emotion, but many. My father experienced sadness, depression, bewilderment, despair, helplessness, loneliness, emptiness, meaninglessness, and probably guilt. All of these are common to grief. What we call grief is a cluster of emotions. We experience them in varying degrees of intensity according to the importance of our loss, and we experience them in no particular order or pattern.

We may wonder if we are losing our minds. Some time ago I spoke about loss and grief to a group of divorced and widowed persons. A woman came up afterward to tell me that she had experienced all the feelings I had described when she lost her husband a year before. She thought there was something wrong with her, that she was losing her mind. She was relieved to know that her actions and feelings were normal. She said she only wished someone had told her so at the time.

Grief can be described as a process of three phases. The first stage is shock, numbness and disbelief. The second is suffering, intense psychic pain. The third is recovery or the completion of mourning. This chapter will deal with the first two stages. The following chapter will treat the third stage and the way a liberal faith can help us in times of grief.

First, some caveats. For the purpose of understanding the emotional dynamics of grief, it is helpful to distinguish three phases of the grieving process. But it should be noted that we do not move automatically from one stage to the next. Sometimes people get stuck in the second stage, suffering, and never get to the stage of recovery. My father was a case in point. Also, the stages overlap. We do not suddenly cease to feel intense psychic pain and one day find ourselves recovered. Moreover, there is no one timetable for the process. We each have our own timetable for each loss we experience. For various reasons when the loss is of a loved one, many find it takes at least a year before they can begin to recover. Usually one has to live through holidays and birthdays and other special days at least once without the loved one, before the intensity of suffering subsides.

A loss may come suddenly, cataclysmically, or gradually, over time, as when someone dies of cancer. When death comes gradually, friends and loved ones may experience what is termed anticipatory grief. That is, they may feel all the emotions of grief in advance of the actual loss. Chronic marital problems over months and years may also give rise to anticipatory grief. However, those who mourn in advance also mourn after loss, though usually not as intensely as do those who experience a sudden loss.

With the caveats that grief seldom follows a systematic sequence and that we may undergo the emotions of grief in many combinations and in differing degrees and forms, we can nevertheless say that grief tends to follow a characteristic pattern.

Numbness

When a significant loss occurs, we experience intense pain and disbelief, but then a kind of numbness sets in as a response to the shock. Numbness protects us from the full impact of our loss by dulling our emotions. Numbness and disbelief keep us from realizing the full extent of our loss. When we first learn that our loved one has died, we usually do not comprehend the full meaning of what we have been told. It takes time to assimilate the terrible news.

May 22, 1982, was a Saturday, and I had agreed to perform three weddings that day. After the first I was home having lunch when I received word that my father had died unexpectedly a thousand miles away. I talked to my sister who lived much closer to our hometown, and we made some necessary decisions. Then I performed the other two weddings and the next morning conducted the Sunday service before flying to Missouri on Sunday afternoon. I could not have done those things in a composed way had I not been protected by numbness, an absence of feeling, and by a lack of full realization that my father was indeed dead.

I see the same phenomenon at work every time I respond to the death of a church member. The bereaved nearly always make the necessary arrangements, help plan the memorial service, and go through the service and reception afterward in a composed manner. People often remark about how well so-and-so did, and they are greatly relieved that they did not have to deal with a weeping, despairing person or family. But in fact the survivors deserve neither credit nor blame. They were able to carry on because they were protected by the perfectly normal and natural initial reaction of numbness.

This phenomenon occurs in other forms of loss as well. A woman told me about her reaction to her divorce. She did quite well for the first several weeks, she said. She went about her work as usual, made a number of important decisions about living arrangements and future plans, and then rather suddenly she was overwhelmed by loneliness, sadness and emptiness.

The Emotions of Grief

Numbness does not last. After a few days or a few weeks, it is replaced by wracking emotions. We feel empty, alone and isolated.[3]

Emptiness, Loneliness, and Isolation. We feel empty because we have lost a part of ourselves. The word *bereavement* comes from *reave* meaning *to be dispossessed*. Something important has been taken away. Each time we lose something or someone, our self is diminished. C.S. Lewis wrote of the death of his wife that it left him feeling like "an empty house." [4] We all receive our identity and our sense of meaning to a great extent from our relationships with others. When our identity is tied very closely to one person, the loss of that person can leave us especially empty, lacking any sense of who we are and what our purpose in life may be. That, I am certain, is what happened to my father.

That also happened to a man I knew who retired from a job of forty years. His work clearly was an important part of who he was as a person. Without it he felt empty within. Mourning the loss of his job, he was mourning the loss of his identity and his sense of being a contributing member of society.

James Carse calls grief a "cosmic crisis," using the word cosmic in its Greek meaning of an ordered world. Because we derive our sense of meaning from our relationships to others and to significant communities, loss, particularly the death of someone close to us, disrupts the order of our world.

> It is not simply that there is one person less to cope with; it is that we live in a universe that makes no sense. The cosmos has lost its fundamental order. As a result, our own lives lose their meaning.[5]

Loss, then, leads us to a spiritual crisis, "a situation in which it is necessary to make a fundamental decision concerning the course and content of our lives." [6] People who suffer a serious loss will have to rebuild their lives, as anyone who has lost a spouse by death or divorce will testify. Loss requires a reaffirmation of the self, sometimes a new definition or a new understanding of who we are. If reaffirmation or new definition does not occur, griefwork cannot be completed.

The grief-stricken person experiences loneliness because she has been cut off from someone she loved. When the loss is of a spouse or member of the immediate family, that person is no longer there in the house with you, no longer there to talk to, to do things with, to eat with. When the loss is of a parent, you may now have the sense that you have been left alone in the world. You are now the older generation of your family.

Loss also brings isolation. The grieving person feels the need to be alone and may even be afraid to go out in public for fear of breaking down. American society does not help in this regard. We don't invite grieving people to social functions because we don't want someone there who might dampen the spirits of others, nor do we want a reminder of death in our presence. We send an unwritten message to the grief-stricken: Stay home until you can resume your normal, all-is-well facade.

Even friends tend to ignore and avoid a grieving person. Being with a grieving person is not pleasant, so we stay away. It is not pleasant in part because it reminds us of death when we prefer to retain our illusion of immortality. Sometimes a grieving person feels lonely and isolated even with others present because others do not understand what she is going through.

Sadness, Depression, and Despair. A move to another city will evoke sadness at the loss of friends and familiar surroundings. Much greater, of course, is the sorrow we feel at the loss of a child or spouse or dear friend. A person in grief has lost something important and yearns for restoration.

Sadness can become depression when our loss is particularly great. We may feel, as my father did, that our lives are over, that there is no longer any reason to live. Ann Kaiser Stearns writes that "for most people, depression is the main feature of grieving and it involves the longest struggle." [7] That is why grieving people are easily fatigued and why it is hard for them to do very much. Depression is terribly tiring.

The lowered energy that results from depression and grief makes it difficult for one to resume a normal work schedule. Again our society is not helpful, for we expect people to resume work within a few days after a significant loss. If a person has major surgery, we do not expect them to return to work the following week, but that is usually what we expect of people who are mourning. The grieving person should be allowed to take several weeks off and then to return to work gradually, part-time at first. It is often good to have work to do, for work gives us some purpose or usefulness and takes our minds off our loss for a while. Work is therapeutic, but only under limited conditions.

Sorrow flows into despair if a person comes to feel that life is futile, that there is no hope for the future, or that he or she can never experience joy or happiness again.

Fear and Anxiety. An early source of anxiety each of us experiences when we are children is the anxiety we feel at the possibility of abandonment. When in later life we lose someone we love and on whom we depend, we feel this anxiety again. It takes the form of concern over whether we can survive emotionally and physically without the other, the terror of helplessness like that we felt as a young child.

Separation from someone to whom we have been close and closely identified with for years can cause us to feel depleted as a person. This is often particularly true for a woman who has heavily invested her life in her husband and his career. If he dies or if they are divorced, she may feel she has lost her own self as well. She may feel deeply anxious about whether she can rebuild her life.

Anxiety is vague and diffuse. Fear is more specific. Divorced persons may specifically fear that they will not be sexually attractive to anyone else. They may fear to venture out alone to social events. The loss of a spouse by death or divorce can produce a feeling of sheer panic about whether you can handle all the tasks of living by yourself. A woman who has never worked outside the home may be frightened about her prospects of getting a job, or scared at the thought of just trying. We may be fearful or anxious about any number of things when we are left alone to cope by ourselves after many years of living with another and depending on that other for support and encouragement. Being left alone can be very frightening, indeed.

Guilt and Self-blame. When we lose someone, we always think of things we might have said or done differently. We think of times when we were thoughtless or unkind or unfair to the one we have now lost. We think of things we wish we had done or said. "Why didn't we take that trip to Europe while she was still able to travel?" "Why didn't I encourage him to take early retirement?"

Survivors may feel guilt related to the manner of death. "Why didn't I insist that he see a doctor sooner?" Or, "It's all my fault; I should have insisted that she get a second opinion." We need to distinguish between realistic and unrealistic guilt. Guilt and self-blame are unrealistic when we are not really at fault for what happened, when we did not actually cause harm to another. And that is most of the time, for most often no one is to blame. Illness and death are chances of nature, the natural result of imperfect physical bodies.

We can always second-guess ourselves, though. We can always think of things we might have done which *might* have made a difference. But the assumption behind many of these thoughts is that we should be perfect, that our foresight should have been as good as our hindsight, that *we* are responsible for the loss. We need to remember that we probably did the things which at the time seemed best, and we need to remember that we can never control another's life. Moreover, had we done the things for which we in grief blame ourselves for not doing, they probably would not have made the hoped-for difference. For all these reasons, such self-blaming thoughts have to be seen as the fruit of unrealistic guilt.

Unrealistic guilt is sometimes related to wishes. As children we believed that wishing could bring something to pass. As adults, if we sometimes wished that an elderly parent who has become a burden were dead, we may feel guilty when the parent does indeed die, as if the wish caused the death. The child whose mother spends so much time with a sick grandparent may wish that the grandparent would die so she can have her mother back. Then when the grandparent does die, the child may feel responsible for the death.

When death occurs in a family, there are many reasons why the children should be included in discussions about the death and the funeral arrangements and should attend the funeral itself. Participation guards against exaggerated guilt the child might feel in regard to the death. Participation also decreases the child's fear and anxiety which may be aroused by the unknowns surrounding death.

Grieving over a divorce, we always think of things we might have done differently. But the primary problem is often a haunting sense of inadequacy. "I made a mess of that relationship; therefore I am a failure. I cannot have a significant relationship with the opposite sex." Here, as so often, friends are important, friends who can help us see that this kind of self-punishment is not grounded in reality.

Realistic guilt issues from something we have done which actually resulted in harm to another. One June morning I was asked to officiate at the funeral of a sixteen-year-old boy accidentally shot by his best friend. They had been

THE HOUR OF LEAD

playing with an "unloaded" handgun, and the friend held it to Robert's head and pulled the trigger.

The boy who pulled the trigger belonged to another church. I did not have the opportunity to help him deal with his guilt. All I could do was advise his father that he might need many sessions with an understanding priest and possibly a therapist. Fortunately the family of the dead boy were very sensitive to the situation. They did everything they could to show that they did not blame their son's friend. Nevertheless, it will not be easy for that young man to make peace with himself, and it will likely take him a long time to do it. He may turn self-destructive to punish himself for the loss he caused.

To be responsible for another's death or disability is a terrible burden. It helps to have loving, understanding, sensitive friends, but it is also important to have a religious faith that can enable us to feel forgiven by that which we hold ultimate. With such a faith as a foundation, we can work on forgiving ourselves.

Anger and Bitterness. When we have lost someone we love, we are understandably angry, and we look for someone or something to blame. We may feel angry at the doctors for what we regard as mistakes they made in diagnosis or treatment. We may be angry at ourselves for not having pushed our loved one hard enough to get a check-up. We may be angry at our lost loved one for leaving us. Though it is irrational, anger at the one we have lost is commonly a part of grief.

We may feel angry at God or fate or, depending on our theology, we may angrily protest the unfairness of the world. Even so devout a Christian as C.S. Lewis expressed rage at God at the loss of his wife.

> If God's goodness is inconsistent with hurting us,
> then either God is not good or there is no God: for
> in the only life we know He hurts us beyond our
> worst fears and beyond all we can imagine.[8]

We can expect to feel angry at whatever we believe to be
ultimate when we lose someone dear. Again, we may be
expressing our sense that we have lost an orderly universe,
that our world has been shattered.

Anger is a normal, natural reaction to loss. We have
cause to be angry; for we have lost someone or something
significant. Anger and resentment are a normal part of the
grief process. If we do not feel anger at some point, we may
be repressing our anger and not dealing with our grief in the
best way. For anger unresolved or unexpressed can lead to
depression, fatigue, irritability, digestive disorders, insomnia,
and other maladies. All of us need an outlet for our anger,
yet it is also important that we not let anger dominate us.

We are increasingly aware that the self is a psycho-
somatic unity; so we should not be surprised that
bereavement affects our physical well-being. A grieving person will often experience symptoms such as loss of appetite,
insomnia, headaches, muscular pain and tightness, weight
loss, fatigue, indigestion, shortness of breath, and tightness
in the throat. In its most acute form grief can actually cause
or at least precipitate death. Thanatologists tell us people
may actually die of a broken heart, as my father did.

The suffering of grief is acute and intense, but it is the
only path to recovery. As John Nichols writes,

> Grieving is putting the world back together again. . .
> . [it] is not, as is commonly believed, the weak side
> of human nature. It is the process by which we
> strengthen ourselves for the task of living coura-
> geously in a universe in which there is very little

security even as there is a great deal of happiness and love.[9]

It is essential that we acknowledge and express our pain, and it is helpful to have good friends to whom we can express it and who will respond in a caring way. Mitchell and Anderson write:

> Crying out one's pain may be largely done alone, but some of that crying needs to be heard and responded to by others who care. Withholding or denying one's feelings will almost inevitably block a person suffering from loss from finding the relief and growth that come with what Granger Westberg has called "good grief." [10]

The role of the liberal religious community is to be among those "others who care," and to that important and many-faceted role we now turn.

9

GOOD GRIEF

When you are sorrowful look again in your heart,
and you will see that in truth you are weeping for
that which has been your delight.

Kahlil Gibran

You cannot prevent birds of sorrow from flying
over your head, but you can prevent them from
nesting in your hair.

Chinese Proverb

The fall is brutal, but we set out again.

Albert Camus

Chekhov wrote a poignant story entitled "Grief" about an old taxi driver in the days when taxis were horse-drawn carriages. The driver's son had died a few days before, and the lonely old driver wants desperately to tell someone the story of his son's illness and death, of the funeral and the terrible loss he feels. He tries to tell his story to all who ride in his taxi, but they are not interested. They do not respond, or they cut him off to talk about something else. Chekhov writes:

> With an anxious and hurried look, he searches among the crowds passing on either side of the street to find if there is just one person who will listen to him. But the crowds hurry by without noticing him or his grief. Should his heart break and the grief pour out, it would flow over the whole earth it seems, and yet no one sees it. It has managed to conceal itself in such an insignificant shell that no one can see it even by day and with a light.[11]

He finally gives up trying to tell his story and ends his day early before he has as many fares as he needs. But he cannot help it. He desperately needs human companionship, and he needs to tell his story to someone. So he goes to the stable hoping to find other cab drivers who will listen. But they are all asleep by the stove. Then he goes out to feed his horse, and there he pours out his soul, telling his story to his horse.

That story movingly depicts one of the most important ways in which we recover from loss and the devastating emotions of grief. We need to let our grief out with others who will hear us. "Give sorrow words," wrote Shakespeare; "the grief that does not speak/Whispers the oe'r fraught heart, and bids it break." [12]

The road to recovery leads through the painful work of grieving, the long and difficult process of experiencing and expressing the emotions discussed in the last chapter. When the loss is a significant one, the suffering is likely to be very intense and very long. Moreover, though we speak of recovery, that is a relative term. The time comes when the worst of the suffering is over, when we are able to resume a more or less normal life, when we once again experience joy in living. But that does not mean we will not at times experience grief again. Many types of grief never wholly end. Something you see or read or something someone says can remind you of your loss, and suffering returns. If you have lost a spouse, each time you see a couple enjoying each other, you are reminded of that of which you have been deprived. If you have lost a child, each time you see a child laughing and playing, you are reminded of what you have lost. If you have lost your health or some part of your body, you will at least occasionally regard healthy and whole people with envy and perhaps resentment.

And grief never wholly ends in the sense that without your lost child or spouse, your life will never return to what it once was. Life may be good again; you may even be happy again, but you will never be the same again. Something valued will always be missing.

Neither is grief healed in a straight line of progress. You can feel better one day and the next regress to an intense degree of suffering, and repeat that alternation many times. C.S. Lewis writes: "One keeps on emerging from a phase, but it always recurs. Round and round. Everything repeats. Am I going in circles. . . ? The same leg is cut off time after time. . ." [13]

Where the loss is of a person — either by death or divorce — the goals of grief work are four: (1) to accept the reality of the loss and its finality; (2) to build a treasured memory; (3) to begin to make new attachments; and (4) to reconstruct a meaningful world.[14] Recovery involves the successful attainment of these goals.

Mourning and Accepting

The values of liberal religion and the ministry of the liberal religious community can be very helpful to persons in reaching these goals. Through religious ceremonies, personal caring and support groups, the religious community is able to encourage and hear the expression of grief and to provide comfort and understanding.

Ceremonies are among the more significant ways in which religion helps grieving persons begin to admit the reality of their loss and to create a cherished memory. Some ministers have developed ceremonies of separation dissolving a marriage for couples or individuals requesting them. Such ceremonies recognize the things which brought the couple together, some of their joys and accomplishments together, the importance of the children if children are involved, and the continued commitment of the parents to the children. They then move to the changes that made separation necessary and to an indication of the future direction their lives will take. A divorce ceremony can help to bring closure to a marriage, thus helping those involved to accept the reality of their changed situation.

Often anger and other emotions are too strong shortly after divorce for such a ceremony. Some have found helpful a ceremony of healing and closure some weeks or months after divorce is legally final. The ceremony marks passage from the status of wife or husband to single person and from one lifestyle to another. It may also include a celebration of the growth that has taken place. Close friends are sometimes invited to attend and even to participate actively.

Upon a death, the funeral or memorial service should be a significant part of the mourning process. Like most religious liberals, I prefer memorial services to funerals. A memorial service usually occurs a week or more after death, and the corpse is not present. In addition to the element of mourning, a memorial service expresses thanksgiving for the life lived, often including statements of appreciation by friends or family members. Different circumstances often mean a difference in tone if not in theme.

Whether one chooses a funeral or a memorial service, cremation or burial, I strongly urge those closest to the deceased to spend some time with the dead body. This can be very helpful in coming to grips with the reality of death. The practice of letting the mortician cremate the body almost immediately after death can hinder acceptance. I know how important it was for my grief work to see the bodies of my parents after death.

Preparation for the service can make a significant contribution to the grieving process. As do most liberal ministers, I always involve family members in helping me plan the service, and this includes talking with me about the deceased. This helps me to prepare the service, but it also assists them in their grief work by helping to begin or continue the creation of a treasured memory of the deceased. What is said at the service by the minister and by others continues the building of a memory. Though the mourners may be still in a state of shock and numbness, they will remember some things said at the service, and these recollections help.

I emphasize two things in the memorial service. First, that we are gathered to mourn a significant loss, and for this I choose readings which evoke feelings of grief, sadness and loss. I strongly disagree with the view that people should not express their grief at services. Quite the contrary, I believe it is very helpful to do so. Certainly, in a religious community the level of trust and understanding ought to be high enough that we should not feel embarrassed by letting our feelings out. The early part of the service gives permission to mourn loss and at the same time helps enable the mourners to accept the reality of their loss.

Later, the memorial service moves from mourning to thanksgiving for the life of the one who has died. The latter half or more of the service is devoted to remembering and celebrating that life. Obviously this adds to what is remembered. Many times something a friend says in the service recalls something loved ones had forgotten or even teaches them something about the deceased they had not known.

Thus the movement of the service is from expression of grief and sorrow to thanksgiving for the life he or she has lived.

In addition to the memorial service, I have developed a participatory ceremony held annually for those who have suffered a recent loss. The ceremony typically takes place on a Sunday afternoon at the end of May near Memorial Day. Most participants have lost a family member within the last year, but some are still mourning losses of earlier years.

I begin the service with some comments about its healing purpose and several readings dealing with the transient nature of life. I then ask each person to light a candle in memory of the one he or she has lost, and say something about what that person meant to him or her. After each has done this, I read selections emphasizing the life of our lost loved ones in our memories and of their influence on us. I then ask each person to say goodbye to their loved one and to snuff out the candle. I conclude with a prayer requesting the grace of healing and the strength to let go. The service is to assist participants to internalize the lost loved one in memory and to let go of their emotional attachment to the person. Deep bonds are also established among some of the participants, who then continue to comfort and help one another in an ongoing way.

We have also celebrated a variation of this at the regular Sunday service on Memorial Day weekend. I invite all who wish to come forward and light a candle in memory of a friend or family member who has died and to say a sentence or two about him or her or simply to acknowledge how much they miss the person. The rest of the service is devoted to the theme of loss and remembrance.

Caring

Liberal religion offers ministries of caring. Here I am speaking not only of the professional ministry but more importantly of the ministry each of us can do for one another. Grief is a lonely work, and no one else can do it for you, but Chekhov was right. Grieving should not have to be done entirely alone. It is important to have others who will listen, empathize, or simply be present in a caring way. Being present to one who has suffered loss can help that person recognize and express feelings. Often there is not much we can say to the grieving. But we can listen to their hurt and confusion. In a time of loss many of us have found, like Chekhov's taxi driver, that no one wants to hear our story. As a community of caring people members of the liberal religious community can be with grieving friends and listen as they tell their story. That is as important when the loss has been by divorce as by death, and when the loss may be of something other than a person.

If a family member has died, it is often helpful especially during the first hours and days simply to free the mourner from routine tasks, such as food preparation, routine shopping, and the tasks of notifying others. Bernadine Kreis and Alice Pattie write:

> As soon as you hear a friend is in grief, phone him. Get to him as quickly as you can. Do not ask him what you can do, ask a member of his family. Once there, be alert. Does he need someone to answer the phone; someone to make calls; send wires; brew coffee; or just sit beside him?[15]

When a person has sustained a great loss, she needs time and space to begin to come to grips with the meaning and reality of that loss. We often urge a mourner to keep busy, but that is not good advice. "Keeping a grieving person busy is really keeping a busy person from grieving." [16]

In his study of *Liberal Religion's Response to Loss*, John Nichols suggests that too often instead of simply being with people and sharing their pain and loss, we tend to feel that we must offer a rational explanation for the loss or address the cause of the loss through social action.

> Rather than help bear the pain and curse the sense-lessness of it all, the liberal will seek for some kind of intellectual precept in a vain attempt to make the unacceptable, more acceptable.[17]

One way we may do this is by offering premature comfort. Our intentions may be very good, but the result is not. For example, when a person has died after a long painful illness, we may try to comfort the bereaved by saying death was really a blessing. That may be true, but it is often heard to mean they should be glad the person died. When someone you loved deeply has gone forever, you are anything but glad. I know when my mother died after a long struggle with cancer, I certainly felt her death was a release from pain for her, but I was bereft. She was my mother, and I did not want well-meaning people in my hometown to tell me it was a blessing. Even so, that was not nearly so bad as hearing them say, again with good intentions but with very bad theology, that it was God's will or that God had called her home.

Saying that the pain will eventually go away is not help-ful either, even though it may be true. Any effort to comfort by short-circuiting the grief process can be harmful because it denies the importance of grieving.

Another unhelpful attempt at premature comfort is to rush to justify the loss or find some meaning in it. "It was God's will," those of traditional religious faith may say.

Religious liberals may suggest that somehow, in ways we do not understand, all things work together for good. But it borders on cruelty to say that to one who has just lost someone very dear, who cannot possibly see any good in what happened.

Ann Kaiser Stearns writes about all attempts to make us feel better:

> We live in a 'fix-it' society, where people think the way to help is to make us feel feelings other than the ones we are actually experiencing. Mistakenly many persons will attempt to offer positive or even cheery words during a time of suffering. What you need instead are friends who can stand alongside you, with patience, while your feelings of sorrow run their course.[18]

Being with one in grief cannot eliminate the sorrow, but it reduces the isolation and anxiety which make grief nearly unbearable. And our caring support should not end with the reception after the memorial service. After the service, when others have gone home, we are needed even more. Then the feeling of isolation and abandonment is greatest. Then the initial shock and numbness have given way to intense suffering. To be aware of this fact and to respond sensitively to it is one of the ways in which a religious community can be especially helpful.

Many churches offer support groups for persons who have known loss. Recently widowed or recently divorced persons can share their experiences and learn from one another how to cope and how to get on with their lives. People who are further along in the grief process can help those in earlier stages. People who have shared the same type of loss can minister to one another and support one another in ways more helpful than can be offered by others who have not had their experience. An example is the Widow-to-Widow program in which a small group of those widowed a year or longer invite people more recently widowed to meet regularly with them to talk about their experience. This kind of support group is often very helpful.

Theological Principles

The theological principles involved in ministry to the grieving include the covenant of the community and what Luther called the priesthood of all believers. Covenant is a Biblical term. It refers to a committed relationship. In the Old Testament God established a covenant with the people of Israel. God and Israel were to be faithful to each other. Israel often broke her covenant with God, but God was always seen as faithful to Israel. Liberal religious communities are covenanted communities in the sense that the liberally religious are bound together in a commitment to shared values, principles and ideals, and to one another. A central principle is the sanctity of each person. This principle means we love and care about one another and are pledged to tend one another's growth and well-being. Our commitment to the principles we share may be represented as the vertical dimension or the God dimension of our covenant. The horizontal dimension involves our commitment to one another. In a covenanted community there are times when the individual subordinates his or her interests to the interests of others or the interest of the whole body of the church.

Religious liberals are for the most part highly individualistic. We think for ourselves and we tend to try to rely on ourselves and ask as little from others as possible. We are self-reliant. These characteristics are among our better virtues, but they sometimes isolate us from others and hinder us from entering into genuine community. Emphasis on our being a covenanted community serves as an antidote to an exaggerated individualism, fear of interdependence, and isolation.

The term *priesthood of all believers* originally referred to Luther's insistence that each person could approach God directly without a priest as mediator. Liberal religion has carried this principle further than more conservative types of religion which still reserve sacerdotal functions for the ordained clergy, for example. But one of the primary functions of a priest is the ministry of healing, and it is this sense of the *ministry of all believers* that applies in the present discussion. Care-giving is not an exclusive preserve of the ordained; it is the responsibility and privilege of all who are in a position to minister.

In chapter one we spoke of the sense of oneness of all creation emerging among many religious liberals. From this awareness of connectedness with others, we experience the empathetic sense of feeling grief when another grieves and of hurting when another hurts. This feeling of connectedness leads to both a covenantal commitment to one another's well-being and a desire to minister to those who mourn. Established on this spiritual foundation of the essential unity of all things and all people, the liberal religious community ought to be a caring community in which we minister sensitively to persons experiencing loss.

Religious liberals also find strength and healing from the deep resources within themselves and within Life, resources which some of us call God. As John Nichols puts it, one strand of liberal religious thought

> recognizes a powerful creative force working in the world, a force which sustains, upholds, comforts and often heals. This force is not immediately available upon the flick of a prayer, but we encounter it when

we know we have reached the limits of our ability to deal with crisis.

This experience of grace involves "a power of healing which flows into individuals whose prior defenses have been torn down by the immensity of their anxiety." [19] But healing power is often mediated through the ministry of caring friends and the ministry of the caring religious community.

Remembering

The end of grieving is emotional release from our attachment to the person we have lost. We attain it by actively making what is lost into a treasured memory. When what is lost is internalized and well-remembered, the bereaved are better able to leave the past behind and take up new emotional involvements in the present once again. Then we can speak meaningfully of recovery.

Because remembering is at first painful, we often resist it. Sometimes caring friends need to encourage the bereaved to reminisce in the knowledge that although it is painful, it does encourage healing. We naturally tend to idealize the lost, but it is important to recollect the negative things too, painful as they may be. None of us is perfect; we shall all leave behind a legacy of failures and hurt as well as a legacy of kindness and generosity and helpfulness. Where divorce is involved, the tendency is to remember only the negative, but it is good to recall positive things about the former spouse as well.

Religious liberals share no consensus on the question of life after death. My own belief is that we live on only in that our words and deeds linger on as influence and as we are remembered by others. (See Part V.) So for me and for many, this matter of remembering the deceased takes on special significance. It is the way in which we give them immortality. It is one last thing we can do for them, to ensure that they live on.

Remembering transfers our image of the person from life to death, from a living person with whom we interact in the present into a person with whom our relationship is now only in the past. Remembering is part of the process of accepting the loss and letting go, so painful but so essential to recovery. It is also a way of affirming that love is stronger than death. For though death can take our loved ones, it cannot take our beloved memory.

Rebuilding

Finally, a person whose life has been shattered by loss needs to come to the point where he or she is ready to resume normal living. This involves restoration and reintegration of a self depleted by loss. The religious community can help in this task in several ways.

If the loss has produced a "cosmic crisis," if it has shattered our sense of an ordered and meaningful world, liberal religion offers help in rebuilding the world. As we noted in the section on meaning, religion has traditionally provided a sense of meaning and purpose to living. Liberal religion's theological or philosophical framework can assist the bereaved in rebuilding a meaningful world.

But though a conceptual framework is essential, it is not enough. Our sense that life has meaning and purpose is mediated to us by others to whom we are of value and importance. By offering support, encouragement and friendship throughout the grieving process, a religious community can help a grieving member retain a sense of self-worth and the sense that life is worth living.

The grief process is not complete until the bereaved has discovered a new purpose for living. The bereaved must choose to live again. A new reason for living may be found in grandchildren, a job, in travel, in volunteer work, or in a thousand places.

Eventually, if we have sufficiently expressed our grief, the time will come when we complete our mourning. The time comes to let go. We already know that from letting go our lesser losses, but we must learn to let go with respect to great losses as well. Life is a drive toward the future, and ultimately we must stop grieving and get on with our lives. It isn't easy, and indeed it is not possible if we have not come through the pain of grieving.

We come through grief a different person, sadder, perhaps wiser, and almost certainly stronger. Colin Parkes says:

> Just as broken bones may end up stronger than unbroken ones, so the experience of grieving can strengthen and bring maturity to those who have previously been protected from misfortune.[20]

Grief is often a door to growth. Sorrow can transform our lives and enable us to be spiritually and emotionally richer. I do not mean to gloss over the tragedy of loss; the tragedy remains. Nor do I mean to suggest that we must suffer loss in order to grow. As I wrote in the previous section, I do not believe everything that happens has a purpose, nor do I believe that what happens to us occurs in order to teach us some kind of lesson. Moreover, it may well be that some grief does not or cannot lead to growth. But this I know: Often grief is a door to growth.

In the aftermath of a very painful divorce, a woman I know examined her life and realized that she had been living a self-centered, shallow and hedonistic life. Dissatisfied with her values and lifestyle, she resolved to change. She joined a Unitarian Universalist Church and adopted personal and spiritual growth as her new goals. Loss and sorrow led to a significant personal transformation that enriched and deepened her life.

Similarly, a woman who lost one of her teen-age sons through suicide began serving as a big sister to motherless children. The excruciating pain she felt as a result of her son's suicide caused her to want to try to heal the hurt of children who had lost their mothers.

It is not comforting to tell a grieving person she will grow from her sorrow. Early in the grief process we should resist making any suggestion that there might be a positive aspect to loss. But it is true that we will not remain the same; we will either be strengthened or weakened by grief.

Grief can even be good in the sense that it can be the road to a new life, not a life we would have chosen had the choice been ours, but a life which we can again love and enjoy.

PART V

THE CRISIS
OF
DEATH

10

LIVING WITH DEATH

We love life; we do not fear death, because we understand that life and death are necessary to each other.

Pearl Buck

Death is not too high a price to pay for having lived. Mountains never die, nor do the seas or rocks or endless sky. Through countless centuries of time, they stay eternal, deathless. Yet they never live! If choice there were, I would not hesitate to choose mortality. Whatever Fate demanded in return for life I'd give, for, never to have seen the fertile plains nor heard the winds nor felt the warm sun on sands beside the salty sea, nor touched the hands of those I love — without these, all the gains of timelessness would not be worth one day of living and of loving; come what may.

Author Unknown

The Denial of Death

From one perspective our lives are tragic because we must all one day die. Whatever we build crumbles; our hopes and dreams eventually end in dust; what we love most, including life itself, we must one day leave behind.

So far as we know we are the only beings aware that we must die, and awareness of death colors and shapes our lives. Samuel Johnson said that the prospect of death wonderfully concentrates the mind. Ernest Becker, in *The Denial of Death*, suggests that

> it does much more than that: the idea of death, the fear of it, haunts the human animal like nothing else; it is a mainspring of human activity — activity

designed largely to avoid the fatality of death, to overcome it by denying in some way that it is the final destiny of [humankind].[1]

We seek immortality, for example, by creating things which will endure beyond our lives — everything from our own offspring to books and buildings. We try to make a place for ourselves in national history or in the history of some institution. We seek to lengthen our lives through medical research and by taking care of ourselves. Of course many religions have offered followers the hope of escape from death, promising some form of immortality.

We inherited the idea of the immortality of the soul from the ancient Greeks. Plato and Socrates taught that human beings consist of a perishable material body and an eternal spiritual substance, the soul. The soul existed before its temporary incarnation in the body, and it would continue to exist in another form after the death of the body. Thus Socrates could calmly drink the hemlock with the assurance that death merely meant a transformation from one form of existence to another.

Early Hebrew religion had no notion of either immortality or resurrection. The human organism was a psycho-physical unity; death meant the end of the individual. The Israelite's hope that his or her life would extend beyond death was grounded in two things: the continuation of life through one's children, and belief in the immortality of the people, that the nation Israel lived on. The idea that God would resurrect the righteous appears in later Judaism, and after contact with Greek thought in the Hellenistic period the notion of immortality enters Jewish religion.

Informed by the Judaic view of human nature, Christianity at first taught the resurrection of the body, apparently meaning the whole person. In this view the soul is not inherently immortal; the whole person dies, body and soul, but God will bring the whole person back to life. Then, with the wedding of Christian theology and Greek philosophy early in the Christian era, the idea of the immortality of the disembodied soul entered Christian thinking.

Today, our scientific-empirical turn of mind has led to widespread skepticism about the survival of individual consciousness. Surveys have shown that most religious liberals do not believe in either resurrection or immortality, or for that matter reincarnation. Many do not have the consolation of believing that death is not the end of our individual lives. However, rather than a disadvantage, I will suggest that this belief can bear positive fruit in our lives. I will also suggest several senses in which our lives do continue after death.

The very language we use to speak of death and dying illustrates our effort to deny the reality of death. We employ euphemisms to avoid using any form of the words *death* or *die*. We say, "She passed away," rather than "She died." Conservative Christians say, "He has gone to his eternal reward." Language both expresses existing attitudes and reinforces them, and our language about death fosters its denial.

And of course many funeral practices are designed to disguise and deny the reality of death. Cosmetics make the deceased look as she did in life; the body is buried in dress clothes to convey the appearance of normality; embalming saves us from ever smelling the odors of death and the rot of its finality; and placing the coffin in a hermetically sealed vault feeds the illusion that the body will never decay — as though the appearance of life could actually sustain life.

We also deny the reality of death by hiding the dying. Modern medical technology has done us an immense service

in extending life, but often its application also means that
the dying are isolated from family and friends. Instead of
spending the last weeks at home, a terminally ill person may
lie in a hospital bed surrounded by life-support equipment or
almost totally sedated. The result is that few of us ever
actually see a person die. We are thus cut off from the
reality of death. Fortunately in recent years, thanks in large
part to the hospice movement, more terminally ill people
have been permitted to return home to die surrounded by
their family and friends.

The refusal of many courts to allow life-sustaining equipment to be disconnected from persons deemed to be in a
"persistent vegetative state" represents still another example
of death-denial.

The only kind of death many people witness is death by
violent means on television shows, news accounts, and mov-
ies. Death is perceptually linked to violence to such a degree
that we may almost convince ourselves that by avoiding
violent death, we can avoid death itself. We subconsciously
assume that death is not a natural event, but only the result
of an accident or of malice. Thus death is associated with
horror and evil. It is not experienced as a beautiful, natural
end to a life well-lived.

Denial of death is powerfully depicted in Tolstoy's little
novel, *The Death of Ivan Ilych*. The novella opens with
Ivan's death after a long illness. Ivan's friends and family
react to his death either as an unpleasant interruption of
their routine, or as a possibility for professional advancement. The friends offer perfunctory expressions of sympathy
to the family. They attend the funeral, but they are not
thinking about Ivan or the meaning of his death but about
their plans for a game of bridge or a meal at a good

restaurant after the funeral. Even in the presence of death, Tolstoy seems to be saying, some will refuse to face it.

The remainder of the novel takes us back through the last years of Ivan's life and also depicts many denials of death. The doctor who treats Ivan never lets on that Ivan may be seriously ill. He brushes aside Ivan's questions about his prognosis, and attends only to his own speculations about the cause of Ivan's illness. As his condition worsens, Ivan's family continues the pretext that he will soon recover. Colleagues who visit refer to the day when he will return to work. No one except a humble servant is honest about his condition. No one except the servant speaks of death or allows Ivan to speak of it. It is as though by not acknowledging it, death will go away. As he slowly realizes that his life is slipping away, Ivan himself repeats the classical syllogism he remembers from grammar school: "All men are mortal; Caius is a man; Caius is mortal." He notes that he never once had thought of it as applying to himself. Caius would die, yes, but not he, Ivan Ilych.[2]

In my experience more and more doctors are being open and honest about the prospects of their terminally ill patients, and that is healthy. It enables the person and the family to prepare both emotionally and in other ways for his or her impending death. Without exception the people I have known who knew they had only a short time to live have been grateful that they had a chance to prepare for their death and have also been able to make the most of their last weeks or months.

From a theological standpoint denial of death is denial of our humanness. To be human is, among other things, to be finite, mortal, limited by death. Acceptance of the reality of death is one aspect of accepting our humanity, and it can be a part of a profound self-acceptance which is the basis for a more creative and fulfilling life.

Denial of death, however, may add to our fear of death. It is a well-known psychological dynamic that thoughts and fears repressed will sooner or later resurface in exaggerated or neurotic forms. Those of us unduly anxious about death (and in a society having generally unhealthy attitudes toward death, that probably includes most of us) can benefit from opportunities to treat death more openly and matter-of-factly.

Such an opportunity came to me several years ago when I taught a college summer session course on "Death and Dying." The course met daily for six weeks, and I found that talking about some aspect of death or dying each day reduced my anxiety about death. I felt the liberating effect of confronting the reality, not only of death in general, but of my own death. Life became more precious. The grass seemed greener, the trees and flowers more beautiful, and I cherished my time with my family and friends more than usual that summer. I wanted to get everything I could from each precious moment, each day, not because I was afraid of dying, but because by facing death, I had become more conscious of life's loveliness. People who have nearly died often respond this way, too.

A religious community can help us deal with the crisis of death and dying in a number of ways, but surely one of the most important is to help us face the reality of death. The religious community can avoid euphemistic language. It can deal with death and dying in worship services and in discussion groups and workshops. To live with the awareness that we shall die is not morbid. Morbidity has to do with debilitating obsession. A simple healthy awareness of reality, however, is liberating. It straightens out our priorities and values. We will still be somewhat afraid and anxious about our own death and the death of those we love. No one who enjoys life and finds it fulfilling wants it to end. No one who loves wants to be separated from those he or she loves. But, accepting the reality of death can help us overcome unhealthy anxiety and can free us to live more productively.

Perhaps just because we do not take the gift of life for granted, our religious faith can help us face death when it comes, less with a sense of loss than with feelings of gratitude for what we have had. That thought is expressed beautifully in this poem.

> And if he die? He for an hour has been
> Alive, aware of what it is, to be.
> The high, majestic hills, the shining sea,
> He has looked upon, and meadows golden-green,
> The stars in all their glory he has seen.
> Love he has felt. This poor dust that is he
> Has stirred with pulse of inward liberty,
> And touched the extremes of hope, and all
> between. . . .[3]

Death and Meaning

What would life be like without death? Most of us might say it would be wonderful. I did when I first put that question to myself. But would it really? The world would become impossibly overcrowded, which would lead to terrible suffering in the form of hunger, poverty, wars over land and resources, and to many other problems. But beyond such fearful speculation, what would our lives be like without the knowledge that we are mortal? Would we have the same incentives to create things of beauty and enduring worth which will outlive us, things that add greatly to the quality of life? Would we have the incentives to live lives that will be memorable because of our good deeds and worthy influence were it not for death? Becker is right. The awareness of death is a mainspring of human activity, and that is not necessarily a negative judgment. It has a positive dimension.

In the children's book, *Tuck Everlasting*, the main characters cannot die. After many years they lose their zest for living, and their lives become boring, monotonous, repetitious and without purpose. They want to die but cannot; life without death is hellish.

Tolstoy's Ivan Ilych shows the value of death in another way. After opening the novel with Ivan's funeral, Tolstoy then writes about Ivan's life. Things had come easily to Ivan. He had risen in the legal profession to a judgeship, a post that paid well and was not demanding. He had married well, though his marriage was devoid of real intimacy and love. His relationship with his children was distant and shallow. He had been concerned primarily with pleasure, social status, and propriety.

Ironically, it was his concern for propriety and social status which led to his undoing. While redecorating his apartment in the most proper and elegant manner possible, Ivan fell and hurt his side. The injury would eventually cause his death. At first his injury did not affect his normal routines of work, playing bridge, and other mundane pleasures such as good food and wine. His work is boring to him, but not difficult, and he prides himself that he knows the "right" people and does the "right" things in his leisure. Tolstoy paints a picture of a self-centered man caught up in trivial pursuits, without any larger purpose, a person not so different from people most of us know, a life Tolstoy describes as "most simple and most ordinary and therefore most terrible." [4]

Only when he begins to rea'
away does he ask what it wɛ
then, for he realizes that hiſ
meaning and without love. '
way of living have been fɛ
and values reflected in tʰ
room. Tolstoy writes,

> In them he saw himself - aḷḷ ᴵ.
> lived - and saw clearly that it waᷤ
> but a terrible deception which had hidaᴧ.
> and death.[5]

He now recognized that his life was a total failure. Like
Mickey Sachs in the movie *Hannah and Her Sisters*, Ivan
did not ask what his life amounted to until he was confronted by death. It is precisely the reality of death that
invites us more compellingly than does any other human
event to deepen our self-understanding and to reach for
greater profundity in our grasp of what it means to be
human. But we need not wait until it is too late as Ivan did.
Recognizing that our lives will some day be over, we may
ask, "How shall I live *now* so that when I die I shall not feel
that I have lived in vain?" Awareness of death can show us
how to value life more highly.

A scene in Thornton Wilder's play *Our Town* poignantly
depicts this point. Emily, a young woman from Grovers'
Corners has died in childbirth. She comes back from the
grave to relive her twelfth birthday. We see her coming
down the stairs on her birthday morning. Her mother greets
her lovingly and comments on each gift as she opens the
packages. Then from off stage we hear her father calling.
Emily is overcome with emotion and says to the Stage
Manager:

n't. I can't go on. Oh! Oh. It goes so fast. We
t have time to look at one another."

e breaks down sobbing.

"I didn't realize. So all that was going on and we
never noticed. Take me back — up the hill — to my
grave. But first: Wait! One more look. Good-by.
Good-by, world. Good-by, Grovers' Corners. . . .
Mama and Papa. Good-by to clocks ticking . . . and
Mama's sunflowers. And food and coffee. And new-
ironed dresses and hot baths . . . and sleeping and
waking up. Oh earth, you're too wonderful for any-
body to realize you."

Then through her tears she asks the Stage Manager:

"Do any human beings ever realize life while they
live it? — every, every minute?"

"No," replies the Stage Manager . . . "The saints
and poets, maybe — they do some." [6]

We do not have to come back from the grave to realize
the preciousness of life and to want, in Kipling's words, "to
fill the unforgiving minute with sixty seconds worth of dis-
tance run." Our awareness that death awaits us can be
enough to deepen our appreciation of life and to affect the
way we live.

Then, when death comes, those of us who have been able
to live well and to accomplish what we set out to do will die
in peace. Satisfaction with what we have done with our lives
makes all the difference in facing death, a point illustrated
by this poem of Holderlin's:

A single summer grant me, great power, and
A single autumn for fully ripened song
That, sated with the sweetness of my
Playing, my heart may more willingly die.

The soul that, living, did not attain its divine
Right cannot repose in the nether world.

But once what I am bent on, what is
Holy, my poetry, is accomplished,

Be welcome then, stillness of the shadows' world!
I shall be satisfied though my lyre will not
Accompany me down there. Once I
Lived like the gods, and more is not needed.[7]

Death gives meaning to our lives in that our awareness of
it pushes us to make the most of the one life we have been
given.

11

BEING HONEST
WITH DEATH

Let it not be a death, but completeness.

Rabindranath Tagore

When we are weary and in need of strength,
  we remember them.
When we are lost and sick at heart,
  we remember them.
When we have joys we yearn to share,
  we remember them.
So long as we live, they too shall live,
  for they are now a part of us,
  as we remember them.

from Jewish service, Yom Tov

Is there not a certain satisfaction in the fact that
natural limits are set to the life of the individual, so
that at its conclusion it may appear as a work of
art?

Albert Einstein

Earlier I referred to the rabbi who said that Unitarian
Universalism did not qualify as a viable religion because it
did not deal with death. I disagree. I believe liberal religion
does deal with death in ways both honest and helpful.

However, whether or not a religious perspective may be
said to deal adequately with death depends largely on what
one considers to be adequate. Some assume that the only
adequate answer to death involves some form of belief in
individual survival after death. It surely consoles many, but
it is surely also *not* the only form of hope or consolation. In
a culture where belief in life after death can no longer be

taken for granted, liberal religion offers other responses to the reality of death. These are bona fide religious responses that are both honest to the critical mind and satisfying to the yearning spirit.

An important element of any honest response to death is the acknowledgement that ultimately, death is a mystery. We do not know and can perhaps never know with certainty what happens after death. We ought to be chary of any religion or philosophy that claims too much. Here as elsewhere the religiously liberal will maintain that the quest for truth is not completed, and that we need to remain open to new discoveries and new possibilities. Whatever else we may say about death or life after death, then, let us begin with the honest affirmation that death is one of life's deepest mysteries.

I suggest three perspectives a liberal faith can affirm which will help us in facing death. First, *death is a natural thing*. In the Garden of Eden story death is seen as a punishment for sin, for when Adam and Eve disobeyed God and ate of the tree of the knowledge of good and evil, they were condemned to return "to the earth from whence they came." In the New Testament Paul refers to "the sting of death." Our culture in general and conservative Christianity in particular have instilled in many of us the sense that death is evil.

Religious liberals by and large understand human life as a part of nature. We regard human nature not as a composite of natural and supernatural elements, but as the highest product of the natural evolutionary process. All things in nature sooner or later die. We accept that. Seeing ourselves as part of the natural world, we can perhaps accept our own deaths more easily. I find it very satisfying to affirm death as nature's way of making room for others, to give others a few years of life on this beautiful earth and to allow us the joy of sharing life with our children, grandchildren, and others. As a natural thing, death cannot be evil; it simply is.

The poet expresses this sense of all life as part of the ongoing process of nature in these words:

> The old log in the woods will never be a great
> tree again . . . things never go back — yet
> lying there — covered with moss — it is
> creating new life — which in turn will be
> great and beautiful. . .

> The fish eats the insect — the bird the fish —
> the mammal the bird — and — the insect the
> mammal — as each — in a universal rhythm is
> creating new life — for there is no life
> except life which comes from life.

> Waters flow where daisies grew —

> Trees grow where swans once swam. . . .

> All things upon this earth are developing into
> new things — from what is here must come what
> is to be . . . there is no other material . . .

> This is the fulfillment of the promise of life —
> nothing can be destroyed — everything is being
> created. . .[8]

The corollary of acceptance of death as a natural thing is a sense of life continuing in the great living whole. Here is a great source of consolation! Shelley expresses this thought beautifully as he writes of his lost friend,

> He is made one with Nature; there is heard
> His voice in all her music, from the moan
> Of thunder, to the song of night's sweet bird; . . .
> He is a portion of the loveliness
> Which once he made more lovely . . .[9]

Liberal religion also offers hope and consolation in the face of death because it teaches that *life and love are stronger than death and hate.* Death is not the meaning of life; the meaning of life is the satisfaction and struggle and triumph of living. We do not have to be immortal to find joy and fulfilment: It is enough to live with courage and dignity.

This theme is poignantly illustrated in Ernest Hemingway's novel *The Old Man and the Sea*. The old man, Santiago, a fisherman, has had a string of bad luck. He has caught nothing for 84 days. It is September and soon the waters will be too rough for frequent fishing. On the 85th day, long before sunrise, the old man sets out once again. This time, determined to find fish, he goes beyond the usual fishing waters, farther out into the sea where the water is deeper and the bigger fish live. He sinks his baited lines down deep, that they might attract a large fish, and indeed it is not long before they do. But the fish on his hook is too large for him to pull in. So he lets it pull him and his little boat farther out to sea. When the fish tires, then he will be able to kill it. The great fish pulls the old man and his boat for two days and two nights in a titanic contest of strength and endurance. The old man cannot sleep, for he must be ever alert in the event the fish should take a sudden dive and pull the boat down with him. With the line around his back, Santiago holds it in one hand so he can take up the slack or give the fish more line. The line cuts his hands and his back. He is bleeding and in pain. But he will not give up until he has caught the fish, or it has killed him.

Finally the fish tires, and Santiago is able to drive his harpoon into its heart. He lashes the fish to the side of the boat and begins the long journey home. He has won his prize; he has done the impossible, alone. With only his stamina, will and intelligence, he has overcome the great fish.

His victory is short-lived though; for soon the sharks come. Unable to repel them, Santiago resigns himself to the fact that they will devour his fish. Eventually he reaches shore and ties up his boat with the skeleton of the great marlin lashed to its side. Exhausted, near death, the old man stumbles up to his shack and falls asleep on his bed of old newspapers.

What have we here? Is this a story of victory or of defeat, a tale of triumph or of the futility of life? To me it is a brilliant and moving parable of the human situation. We struggle and sacrifice and give all we have, apparently only to lose it in the end. But in fact we do not lose what is really important. The old man lost his fish, but neither death nor the sharks could take away the satisfaction of his efforts or the triumph of his victory. It does not matter that the old man returned with only a carcass. From a material standpoint, the carcass was worthless, but spiritually it was everything. For it represented the triumph of the human spirit against great odds.

To me the story is a great modern parable of the victory of life over death. The old man will die, but it does not matter because his life has meaning and purpose. He has accomplished what he set out to accomplish. Santiago says it well, "Man is not made for defeat. . . A man can be destroyed, but not defeated." [10]

It is not the material results of life that are important. Not what we accumulate, not what we save, not even the list of achievements we can point to. What counts is the living — the seeking, striving, risking, suffering, the capacity to live our days to the fullest.

And to love. There is a great deal of love in *The Old Man and the Sea*. Santiago loves the sea and he loves the fish. He calls the fish his brother. He does not want to kill it, though he must. His love for nature is deep and sustaining. There is also deep love between the old man and the boy whom he has taught to fish and who cares for Santiago, bringing him food and coffee and bait. And this love, too, sustains them both.

Life and love are stronger than death. As long as the human spirit rises to the challenge of each new day and each new epoch, as long as we pursue worthwhile goals, as long as we strive, struggle, suffer and endure, just so long do we find joy and fulfilment. As long as we give ourselves to each other in love, just so long do we find meaning and satisfaction. In these ways we prove that life is stronger than death.

Finally, liberal religion can offer a kind of immortality: *we are immortal in the sense that who we are and what we do lives on after we die.* Occasionally I am asked to conduct a funeral or memorial service for someone I did not know. In that situation, I always meet with the family before I prepare the service so that I can get a better sense of the person whose life we are commemorating. I ask family members to tell me about him or her. As I listen to them speak of their deceased mother or father or wife or husband, I often have a strong sense that the dead person continues to be a very real and important presence in their lives. After the service I am often told that my words suggested that I knew him or her well, and I sometimes reply, "I did, though I only met her (him) after she (he) died."

Our influence lives on after our death.

> Were a star quenched on high
>   For ages would its light
> Still traveling downward from the sky
>   Shine on our mortal sight.

> So, when a good person dies,
>   For years beyond our strife
> The light he or she leaves behind
>   Shines on our common life.[11]

We experience immortality in the sense that our spirit and our influence live on. And this suggests that the kind of life we live is terribly important. For if we live on through the lives we touch, then the ways we touch the lives of others is what really matters. In a word, it is precisely what we are able to give of ourselves to others that lives on after we die. What we keep dies with our body. A fundamental truth of human existence is that we transcend death insofar as we live in and through each other.

Robert G. Ingersoll wrote,

> Let us believe that pure thoughts, brave words, and generous deeds can never die. Let us believe that a noble self-denying life increases the moral wealth of [humankind], and gives assurance that the future will be grander than the past.

Our giving to one another has a ripple effect, like a stone thrown into the water. The ripples continue to be seen in ever-widening circles long after the stone has dropped from sight. So our lives may continue to influence the world long after we have gone to our graves.

Through organ donation or the donation of our bodies to medical research, modern medical technology offers many of us a tangible way to make our lives count beyond death. The donation of a good organ can save and extend another's life, and the donation of one's body to research may also indirectly help others. Where either of these is a possibility, it becomes an ethical imperative for those who care about others.

The liberal religious community plays an important role in enabling us to live on in memory and influence. It provides opportunities for service to others. In that way our impact on the world is increased. The community also provides ways in which we can be remembered, in a memorial service and also at later times, at a service on Memorial Day weekend, for example. This passage from the Jewish *Yom Tov* service speaks eloquently of the role played by the living in immortalizing the dead:

> When we are weary and in need of strength,
>   we remember them.
> When we are lost and sick at heart,
>   we remember them.
> When we have joys we yearn to share,
>   we remember them.
> So long as we live, they too shall live,
>   for they are now a part of us,
>   as we remember them.

"All this is well and good," I can imagine someone saying, "with respect to those who are granted long life. But what about the death of children? What kind of hope or consolation does liberal religion offer to the parents of a dying child, or to the child herself?"

What consolation can any religious teaching give? Even the promise of another life beyond death will not bring back the child nor ease the pain of separation and loss. Some forms of traditional religion add an awful burden by implying that untimely death may be a punishment of God on the parents. Religious liberals find this repugnant.

When a child dies, the liberally religious offer the consolation of caring friends and a faith that a short life is better than no life, and has meaning. These words, written by a grief-stricken father and read at the funeral of his fifteen-year-old son killed in a shooting accident, express these thoughts.

> Rob, you have had a happy and productive fifteen years. You have added to our lives as we have added to yours . . . Your life has been worth living even though it was shorter than we would have liked. Even in death you have helped at least two others live a better life by donating portions of your body.

The family had donated the boy's heart and liver. And in lieu of flowers they had requested that donations be made to a group lobbying for stricter gun-control legislation. Through these, too, they were able to think of their son's death as not having been in vain.

At whatever age death may come, I find it helpful to think of ourselves, not as totally discreet and separate beings, but as part of a Great Living System or, to change the metaphor, a Great Stream of Life. Earlier I wrote of the new myth of the unity of all things. According to that myth, birth is our emergence onto the surface of the great stream of life and death is our re-emergence back into the whole. Within this context life is the time when we have individual conscious being, and opportunity to enrich the whole. Upon our death, we no longer exist as self-conscious individuals, but we are still a part of the whole.

With a profound sense of both our unity with all things and our continuing presence in the world, Tom, the union organizer in John Steinbeck's *The Grapes of Wrath*, memorably says good-by to his family:

> "Maybe . . . a fella ain't got a soul of his own, but on'y a piece of a big one — an' then — "
>
> "Then what, Tom?"
>
> "Then it don't matter [if I die]. Then I'll be all aroun' in the dark. I'll be ever'where — wherever

you look. Wherever they's a fight so hungry people can eat, I'll be there. Wherever they's a cop beatin' up a guy, I'll be there. . . I'll be in the way guys yell when they're mad an' — I'll be in the way kids laugh when they're hungry and they know supper's ready. And when our folks eat the stuff they raise, and live in the houses they build — why, I'll be there. See? . . .[12]

Even the great rationalist Bertrand Russell expresses this idea when he writes:

An individual human existence should be like a river — small at first, narrowly contained within its banks — then rushing passionately past boulders and over waterfalls. But, gradually, as the river grows wider, the banks recede, the waters flow more quietly, and, in the end, without any visible break, they become merged in the sea, and painlessly lose their individual being.

Death is one of the deepest mysteries we human beings face. We cannot say with assurance what lies beyond this life. We can affirm with certainty that those able to live in such a way that their lives count, those who give of themselves in deeds of love, those who act in behalf of justice and mercy, attain a sense of life that knows no death. If we live like that we attain a genuine immortality like that celebrated in these familiar lines of George Eliot's poem:

Oh, may I join the choir invisible
Of those immortal dead who live again
In minds made better by their presence; live
In pulses stirred to generosity,
In deeds of daring rectitude, in scorn
For miserable aims that end with self,
In thoughts sublime that pierce the night like stars,
And with their mild persistence urge men's search
To vaster issues. So to live is heaven:
To make undying music in the world . . .[13]

The measure of our lives is not the length of our years, not the quantity of life, but the quality of our living. Paradoxically, the better we live the more likely we are to be able to regard death not as an enemy but as "the last stage of life." (Elizabeth Kubler-Ross)

We have come full circle again. We have spoken of a liberal religious understanding of the meaning of life in terms of the contribution we make to the world and in a larger sense to the ongoing evolution of the Great Living System. Our awareness of being part of and contributing to the Great Living System can enable us to accept death with serenity and a sense of completion. Ours is the faith that our lives are not lost or meaningless. We are part of an ongoing, perhaps eternal process. Our faith makes it possible to face death with courage and with thanksgiving for having been given the splendid gift of life.

NOTES

PART I: The Nature and Resources of Liberal Religion

1. "Culture," *Encyclopedia of the Social Sciences*, Vol. IV, pp. 641-642, cited by John Ruskin Clark, *Highroad to Advance*, ed. Irving R. Murray, Pacific Grove, CA: Boxwood Press, 1976, p. 3.

2. Dag Hammarskjold, *Markings*, New York: Alfred A. Knopf, 1964, p. 56.

3. There are many excellent books dealing with theology from a feminist perspective. For an especially interesting discussion of the differences between male and female symbolism of deity, see Riane Eisler, *The Chalice and the Blade*, San Francisco: Harper and Row, 1988.

4. Albert Einstein, *Cosmic Religion, with Other Opinions and Aphorisms*, New York: Covici-Friede, 1931. Quoted by Judith Walker-Riggs, "A Cosmic Theology," in *What Unitarian Universalists Believe: Living Principles for a Living Faith*, The Unitarian Universalist Denominational Grants Panel, 1987, p. 74. Emphasis added.

5. Alice Walker, *The Color Purple*, New York: Washington Square Press, 1982, p. 177-8.

6. Alice Walker, *op. cit.*, p. 178.

7. Antoine de Saint Exupéry, *Wind, Sand and Stars*, New York: Reynal and Hitchcock, 1939, pp. 26-32.

PART II: The Crisis of Meaning and Purpose

1. Albert Camus, *The Myth of Sisyphus*, New York: Vintage Books, 1960, p. 3.

2. Carl G. Jung, *Modern Man in Search of a Soul*, New York: Harcourt, Brace and World, 1933, p. 61.

3. Mario Cuomo, quoted by Judy Mann, *The Washington Post*, June 14, 1985, p. B-3.

4. Dean M. Kelley, *Why Conservative Churches Are Growing*, San Francisco: Harper and Row, 1977, p. 38.

5. Paul Tillich, *The Courage To Be*, New Haven: Yale University Press, 1952, p. 47.

6. Viktor Frankl, *Man's Search for Meaning*, New York: Washington Square Press, 1963, p. 154.

7. Richard S. Gilbert, *The Prophetic Imperative*, Boston: Unitarian Universalist Asociation, 1980, p. iii.

8. Quoted by Harold S. Kushner, *When All You've Ever Wanted Isn't Enough*, New York: Summit Books (Simon and Schuster), 1986, p. 143.

9. Harold S. Kushner, *op. cit.*, p. 39.

10. *Ibid.*, p. 42.

11. Ecclesiastes 9:7-10, quoted and translated by Kushner, *op. cit.*, pp. 139-140.

12. Kushner, *op. cit.*, p. 143.

13. Saul Bellow, *Mr. Sammler's Planet*, Greenwich, Conn.: Fawcett Publications,Inc., 1970, p. 215.

14. C.G. Jung, *op. cit.*, pp. 109-110.

15. Gilbert, *op. cit.*, p. iii.

16. H.Richard Niebuhr, *Radical Monotheism and Western Culture*, New York: Harper and Row, 1964, pp. 118-9.

17. Alfred Adler, *What Life Should Mean to You*, New York: Capricorn Books, 1958, pp. 8-9. Italics added.

18. Cuomo, *op. cit.*

19. Florence van Straten, "Giving Life New Meaning," *Unitarian Universalist World*, April 15, 1986, p. 5.

20. John Steinbeck, *The Grapes of Wrath*, New York: Viking Penguin Books, 1976, p. 105.

21. Frederick Witt Gilkey, unpublished talk given at River Road Unitarian Church, February, 1989. Used with author's permission.

22. As paraphrased by John Ruskin Clark, *The Great Living System*, Boston: Skinner House, 1977, p. 80.

23. George Wald, "Theological Resources from the Biological Sciences," *Zygon* 1, 1966, pp. 46-7. Quoted in John Ruskin Clarke, *op. cit.*, pp. 82-3.

24. Brad Lemley, "Biodance", *Washington Post Magazine*, February 23, 1986, p. 10.

25. Norman Cousins, "Litany for Moderns," in *Readings for Common Worship*, Boston: Unitarian Universalist Association, 1981, p. 3.

26. Quoted by Judith Walker-Riggs, *op. cit.*, italics added.

27. *Essay on Man*, as quoted by John Ruskin Clark, *op. cit.*, p. 68.

PART III: The Crisis of Pain and Suffering

1. Archibald MacLeish, *J.B.*, Boston: Houghton Mifflin Company, 1958, p. 111.

2. Fyodor Dostoevsky, *The Brothers Karamasov*, New York: Random House, 1950, p. 289.

3. Albert Camus, *The Plague*, New York: The Modern Library, 1948, pp. 196-197.

4. F. Forrester Church, *The Devil and Dr. Church*, San Francisco: Harper & Row, 1986.

5. G. Peter Fleck, *The Mask of Religion*, Buffalo: Prometheus Books, 1980, pp. 74-75.

6. David W. Angevine, unpublished letter to the author; used by permission.

7. John B. Cobb, Jr., and David Ray Griffin, *Process Theology: an Introductory Exposition*, Philadelphia: The Westminster Press, 1976, p. 53.

8. Anthony Friess Perrino, *Holyquest: The Search for Wholeness*, Carmel, CA: Sunflower Ink, p. 57.

9. Viktor E. Frankl, *op. cit.*, p. 179.

10. *Ibid.*, p. 164.

11. Max Coots, *Seasons of the Self*, Nashville: Abingdon Press, 1971, p. 24.

12. William F. Schulz, in "Unitarian Universalist Views of Suffering," pamphlet published by the Unitarian Universalist Association, Boston, MA., p. 10.

13. J.B., *op. cit.*, pp. 151-152.

14. *Ibid.*, p. 153.

15. Emile Durkheim, *Elementary Forms of the Religious Life*, 1912, as paraphrased by Harold S. Kushner, *When Bad Things Happen To Good People*, New York: Schocken Books, 1981, p. 118.

16. *J.B.*, *op. cit.*, p.153.

17. From the "Purposes and Principles of the Unitarian Universalist Association" adopted in 1985.

18. *The Brothers Karamasov*, *op. cit.*, p. 616.

19. Dorothy Soelle, *Suffering*, Philadelphia: Fortress Press, 1975.

PART IV: The Crisis of Loss and Grief

1. Kenneth R. Mitchell and Herbert Anderson, *All Our Losses, All Our Griefs*, Philadelphia: The Westminster Press, 1983, p. 51.

2. Judith Viorst, *Necessary Losses*, New York: Simon and Schuster, 1986.

3. This discussion of the emotions of grief is particularly indebted to the excellent discussion in Mitchell and Anderson, *op. cit.*, pp. 61-82.

4. C.S. Lewis, *A Grief Observed*, New York: Bantam Books, 1976, p. 13.

5. James P. Carse, "Grief as a Cosmic Crisis," Otto S. Margolis, et al., editors, *Acute Grief: Counseling the Bereaved*, New York: Columbia University Press, 1981, p. 5.

6. *Ibid.*

7. Ann Kaiser Stearns, *Living Through Personal Crisis*, New York: Ballantine Books, 1984, p. 88.

8. Lewis, *op. cit.*, p. 31.

9. John H. Nichols, *Liberal Religion's Response to Loss*, Boston: The Minns Lectures, 1985, p. 2.

10. Mitchell and Anderson, *op. cit.*, p. 96.

11. Anton Chekhov, "Grief", in Mary Jane Moffat, ed., *In the Midst of Winter*, New York: Random House, 1982, p. 28.

12. *Macbeth*, Act 4, Scene 3.

13. C. S. Lewis, *op. cit.*, p. 67.

14. Paraphrased from Mitchell and Anderson, *op. cit.*, p. 110.

15. Bernadine Kreis and Alice Pattie, *Up From Grief*, Minneapolis: The Seabury Press, 1969, p. 94.

16. Mitchell and Anderson, *op. cit.*, p. 114.

17. Nichols, *op. cit.*, p. 55.

18. Stearns, *op. cit.*, p. 14.

19. Nichols, *op. cit.*, p. 47.

20. Colin Parkes, quoted by Charles S. Stephen, Jr., "Living with Grief," *CLF News Bulletin*, October, 1977, p. 5.

PART V: The Crisis of Death

1. Ernest Becker, *The Denial of Death*, New York: The Free Press, 1973, p. ix.

2. Leo Tolstoy, *The Death of Ivan Ilych*, New York: New American Library, 1960, p.131f.

3. Arthur Davison Ficke, "Tumultuous Shore", quoted in Carl Seaburg (ed.), *Great Occasions*, Boston: Beacon Press, 1968, p. 269.

4. Tolstoy, *op. cit.*, p. 104.

5. *Ibid.*, p. 152.

6. Thornton Wilder, *Our Town: A Play in Three Acts*, New York: Harper and Row, 1957, pp. 99-100.

7. Quoted by Walter Kaufmann, *The Faith of a Heretic*, Garden City, New York: Doubleday Anchor Books, 1963, p. 367.

8. Author unknown.

9. Percy Bysshe Shelley, "Adonais," in *A Treasury of Great Poems*, ed. Louis Untermeyer, New York: Simon and Schuster, 1942, p. 742.

10. Ernest Hemingway, *The Old Man and the Sea*, New York: Charles Scribner's Sons, 1952, p. 103.

11. Author unknown.

12. John Steinbeck, *The Grapes of Wrath*, New York: Viking Penguin Books, 1976, p. 537.

13. George Eliot, "The Choir Invisible," in *101 Famous Poems*, Chicago: Henry Regnery Co., 1958, p. 137.